A Mother's Time

A Mother's Time

Elise Arndt

While this book is intended for the reader's personal enjoyment and profit, it is also intended for group study. A Leader's Guide with Victor Multiuse Transparency Masters is available from your bookstore or from the publisher.

VICTOR BOOKS®

A DIVISION OF SCRIPTURE PRESS PUBLICATIONS INC.
USA CANADA ENGLAND

Unless otherwise noted, Scripture quotations are from *New American Standard Bible*, © the Lockman Foundation 1960, 1962, 1963, 1968, 1971, 1972, 1973, 1975, 1977. Verses marked TLB are taken from *The Living Bible*, © 1971, Tyndale House Publishers, Wheaton, IL 60189. Used by permission. Verses marked AMP are taken from *The Amplified New Testament*, © 1954, 1958 the Lockman Foundation. Verses marked KJV are taken from the *King James Version*.

Recommended Dewey Decimal Classification: 301.412 6
Suggested Subject Heading: MOTHERS

Library of Congress Catalog Card Number: 87-81021
ISBN: 0-89693-338-5

DEDICATION

To my husband, Warren, my constant source of encouragement. Your faith in me, your love, and your patience were so real. Thank you for being God's special touch in my life.

Contents

ACKNOWLEDGMENTS

Writing a book is always a big undertaking, and it is especially so when you have a four-year-old child. In the process of making the commitment to write again, I asked the Lord to provide a way it could be done without Danny being neglected. God is faithful! He provided many people to accomplish His purpose in my life.

Many thanks to the following: all those who prayed faithfully and shared the vision of *A Mother's Time*; Sherine Wakim, a young girl who occupied Danny in my home so I could work a few extra hours uninterrupted; Barb Feys, who from the beginning of my writing offered to care for Danny and prayed me through the rough days; Joyce Davis, who so often saw in me what I could not see in myself; Faye Colando, for typing the manuscript; my husband, Warren, for his many hours of reading and editing; and my children, Paul, David, Liz, John, and Danny, for their sense of humor and constant help and support.

Chapter 1

The Mysterious Gift of Time

Without a doubt, it was those years our family spent as missionaries in the mountains of New Guinea that taught us a concept of time quite different from that of the Western world. New Guinea was a place out of the ordinary. Our environment consisted of majestic mountains, lush green foliage, waterfalls streaming from the face of mountains, and deep valleys lying in stillness. It was as if God's splendid creation was suspended in time.

New Guinea has been referred to as "the land that time forgot." After living in this cultural setting for many years, we can attest to the truth of that saying. The Ipili people of the Pogera (an area located deep in the mountains) were literally untouched by modern technology. One of their greatest moments of progress came when their stone axes were replaced with steel ones. Life in this isolated area of the world had been as we found it for centuries. It seemed that time really did stand still.

In this society, void of great technological advancements, I was able to see God's creation and His concept of time from a

11

new perspective. No skyscrapers or jets obstructed my view of the vivid blue sky, a sky untainted by pollution. The evenings were so still I could hear every twig snap. Television and the telephone were foreign to that society.

Entertainment consisted of playing games, reading, sewing, writing letters, or simply talking with one another. Often I was compelled to stop what I was doing and enjoy the majesty of God that I saw in the sunsets, mountains, and people. What special moments I had sitting with the Ipili women! As they worked with their hands, weaving net bags and loincloths, at times we talked for hours. No one watched a clock or seemed to be in a hurry. During those times together, I learned to love and appreciate these sincere, gentle women who taught me much about mothering and life in general.

SO MUCH TO DO!

In contrast to the simplicity that surrounded me was the complexity of living in a primitive society. My days were anything but slow moving and uneventful. From tribal warfare to delivering babies and taking care of my family, I was *busy*. I had four preschool children. That, in itself, would keep any mother of any culture active.

My day began with the rising of the sun. I spent hours in the kitchen preparing meals on a wood-burning stove. Everything was made from scratch—bread, tomato sauce, puddings, cakes, and even marshmallows and potato chips.

Clothes were washed in an antiquated, hand-pump washing machine. Water was heated in a large copper kettle over an open fire. Just hauling it to those large galvanized tubs was a big job.

My duties were not limited to my home. I had gardens and chickens to care for. There was always an endless stream of Ipili people who needed my immediate attention. Working in the medical clinic and teaching women hygiene, sewing, literacy, prenatal and postnatal care, and the Bible were all part of a normal day. Relief came in the evenings with the setting of the sun. The New Guinean's day stopped and so did ours. We withdrew to our homes and there relaxed, retiring early.

Our adjustment to the Ipili way of life was not easy. We entered this culture with new Timex watches on our wrists and the Western world's concept of time in our heads. We were accustomed to schedules regulated by clocks. The Ipili people's guide to time was the sun and the seasons of the year.

Nothing ever began on time—*our* time, that is. Delay after delay brought us to the point of exasperation. To the New Guinean it was not a problem that needed correcting. We were the ones who needed to change and adjust to a new way of life.

Beginning anything on time meant waiting until everyone had arrived. Church on a Sunday morning would begin anywhere from 9 A.M. to noon. Needless to say, it took me a while to catch on to this.

I tried hard to make Sunday a unique day for my family. I planned special dinners and dressed the children in their very best. At 9 o'clock we were ready, but that didn't mean it was time to begin.

Outside the church, clusters of men and women were seated on the ground talking. The sound of their chatter made it quite apparent they were having a good time. Could it be that they were more interested in socializing than worshiping?

My husband, Warren, would ask Andele, our native evangelist, if he could begin church. Andele would reply, "Not yet. So-and-so isn't here. We have to wait." One hour would pass and then two. *Don't these people understand that I have things planned for the afternoon?* I would think. My roast was going to burn, and my children's Sunday clothes would soon get dirty.

It was fruitless to try to change the people to fit our schedule of dinner and clean children. The old saying goes, "If you can't beat 'em, join 'em," and that is exactly what we did.

My children got dirty; Elisabeth's little white ruffled dress never did recover from the embedded dirt. And my roasts got well done until I learned to change my schedule. What we gained as a result were cherished moments shared with God's people.

LIFE BY THE CLOCK

In 1972 our family arrived back in the United States. For five years we had not allowed a clock to rule our lives. What a shock to return to such a time-oriented culture! At first we rebelled against the frustrations of being controlled by a clock. But once again we adapted to the prevailing culture's concept of time.

Even with all the modern conveniences at my disposal—gas stove, washer, dryer, grocery stores, telephone, car, and a modern, efficient home with all types of appliances and gadgets—I struggled with getting things done. Time began to be a real problem. There was never enough of it.

Staying up later and rising earlier became a way of life. Reading good literature was becoming a thing of the past. The TV became a great interference in family communication, and the telephone constantly intruded into our private life. Where once evenings were times to relax and regroup for the next day, now they were filled with church meetings, Bible studies, P.T.A. meetings, and extracurricular activities for the children.

Where were the times for enjoying sunsets? What was happening to those quiet evenings spent with the family? Everyone seemed so busy doing his own thing.

One day I came across Job 7:6: "My days are swifter than a weaver's shuttle, and come to an end without hope." That was exactly how I felt. Disorganization began to creep into my life. Confusion and frustration reigned.

Something had to change! I knew in the midst of busyness there could be time for capturing a moment; for building memories; for enjoying quiet moments with my Lord, my family, and others. I had experienced that in the midst of a busy life in New Guinea. It was not beyond my grasp here in the United States.

After much soul-searching, I realized that two important values had changed since my return. First, I found, the years I spent among the Ipili people were filled with an intimate relationship with Jesus Christ. He was first in my life. I depended on Him. My day began with Him, continued and ended with Him. Now there were so many other things I could lean on to meet my needs. Doctors were only a phone call away. Stores were available to me at every turn. Other people were always present for a listening ear. My need for God began to dwindle.

The second big change came in the area of craving the "things of this world." In New Guinea, life did not consist in the abundance of things. I found satisfaction and joy in people. I was thankful for our adequate home and furnishings, but upon returning I felt little remorse in having to leave behind my material possessions. The reason my heart broke was that we had to leave people we had grown to love.

Once back, however, it did not take me long to lose the proper perspective on life. I was dazzled by the American way. The world was like a candy shop, and I was a little girl peering through the window. I wanted it all. My priorities became jumbled. I lost control, and the desires of my flesh began to rule.

My desire for material things began to crowd out the spiritual. Time alone with my Lord was replaced by the activity of serving Him. Making sure my children had the "best of everything" crowded out time spent with them.

My time problem boiled down to a problem with self and the sin of greed. Colossians 3:2 and 5 say: "Set your mind on the things above, not on the things that are on earth. . . . Therefore consider the members of your earthly body as dead to . . .

greed, which amounts to idolatry." My life was slowly being bound up in materialism. How I praise and thank God for His patience and love in teaching me the only way of living a productive life! He never let go of me in all my striving.

Our highly technological and materialistic society has become a great deterrent to our enjoying an intimate relationship with our Lord and other people. One would think that with all the time-saving devices available, we would have hours at our disposal for relaxation and pleasure. Just the opposite is true. Extra hours become filled with activity and complaining.

Each of us has been granted the same 24-hour day. No one has been cheated. The sun rises and sets on the wicked as well as the righteous (Matt. 5:45). Why is it that people have such a problem with time management? Why do some accomplish so much and others so little? Why are some enjoying life while others are frazzled, bound to schedules, and losing perspective on what life is really about?

GOD CREATED TIME

Time is one of the most precious earthly commodities given to us by the Lord. With the passing of each day, 86,400 seconds disappear, never to be recaptured. As one of God's gifts, time is also one of His mysteries.

Although God is infinite and timeless, He chose to create a world governed by time. His own Son, Jesus, was sent in time to the earth and restricted Himself to time's strictures.

Recently I heard a commercial for a watch company that went something like this: "Man invented time, but Seiko perfected it." God did give man the knowledge of measuring time with hours and seconds, but man did not invent it. God was the Creator and is still the Controller of it.

Genesis 1:1 says, "In the beginning." Our infinite God uses a mark of time to describe His creative process. In Genesis 1:5 we see the description of the first 24-hour day. "And God called the light day, and the darkness He called night. And there was evening and there was morning, one day." With the division of light and darkness came "one day." Then, on the fourth day, the sun, moon, and stars were created.

In Genesis 1:14-15 we see God's purpose in creating these heavenly bodies.

> Then God said, "Let there be lights in the expanse of the heavens to separate the day from the night, and let them be for signs, and for seasons, and for days and years; and let them be for lights in the expanse of the heavens to give light on the earth"; and it was so.

God's order was evident. Everything He created had a unique purpose. The vastness of the universe with its millions of heavenly bodies was designed to give earth signs, seasons, days, years, and light.

Into God's sinless, perfect world He brought time. In the beginning, time was not a problem for God or the people He created. It was a mark of His orderliness. It was the way He wanted His world to exist in perfect harmony. The sun, moon, and stars were created not just for beauty and light, but for order.

When man was placed into this orderly world, he was given an overwhelming responsibility: "Then the Lord God took the man and put him into the garden of Eden to cultivate it and keep it" (Gen. 2:15). The Lord also gave Adam the enormous task of naming every living creature: "whatever the man called a living creature, that was its name" (Gen. 2:19). Truly, Adam was a busy man.

TIME AFTER THE FALL

It wasn't until sin came into the world, however, that time and work became a problem. God had to speak harshly to Adam:

Cursed is the ground because of you;
In toil you shall eat of it
All the days of your life.
Both thorns and thistles it shall grow for you;
And you shall eat the plants of the field;
By the sweat of your face
You shall eat bread. (Gen. 3:17-19)

With that Fall came man's problems with time: the use and abuse of it and the constant search to try to "save" it. How does one go about doing that? Can you store it in a bottle or deposit it in a bank, later to be drawn out? One of the mysteries about time is that it never returns. It is usable only as it is received and once used it is lost forever. You only have to take a look at the aging process to realize that the years which have passed will never return. They are gone. We have only one time to live life. We can live it God's way—abundant, or full (John 10:10)—or according to the desires of the flesh, which only leads to destruction (Rom. 8:6). We have the choice!

"Let a man regard us in this manner, as servants of Christ, and stewards of the mysteries of God. In this case, moreover, it is required of stewards that one be found trustworthy" (1 Cor. 4:1-2). Being a good steward of this mysterious gift of time is what God requires. Will we be found trustworthy in the management of it?

Ephesians 5:15-17 commands us to be wise.

Look carefully then how you walk! Live purposefully and worthily and accurately, not as the unwise and witless, but as wise—sensible, intelligent people; making the very most of the time—buying up each opportunity—because the days are evil. Therefore do not be vague and thoughtless and foolish, but understanding and firmly grasping what the will of the Lord is. (AMP)

18

"So teach us to number our days," the psalmist says, "that we may present to Thee a heart of wisdom" (Ps. 90:12).

We know what God expects of us—to live purposeful, worthy, accurate lives; being wise and making the most of our time. Yet we struggle with living in a world that seeks to devour us. Stress and pressure have entered our world as a result of sin, and with sin also come physical and mental anguish.

The remedy to the time management problem goes a lot deeper than learning how to "save" time. It is a spiritual problem that cannot be corrected merely by external means. We must come to grips with ourselves and the sin dwelling within us. By confessing our sin before God and submitting to the lordship of Jesus Christ, we allow the Holy Spirit to instruct us in the proper use of our time.

I know extremely organized people. They have their lists of things to do and goals set. Their lives progress in an orderly, efficient way from one activity to the next. I greatly respect people who live such disciplined lives. But there is a dangerous trap into which many fall. We can be so strictly scheduled that we entirely miss the importance of people and a relationship with God.

THE VIRTUOUS WOMAN

The woman described in Proverbs 31 is one of those amazingly efficient women. Her life must have been filled with order. As a young mother, I was convinced this outstanding woman never experienced four preschoolers at one time. She couldn't have accomplished what she did with four pairs of eager hands "helping" her. Could I ever be like her? I knew she was God's model for my life, but at age 27 I became weary just reading about all she accomplished.

When I read about her as a mother of four older children I was more than convinced that she had never experienced raising four teenagers at one time. It's recorded at the end of

19

Proverbs 31 that her children actually rose and called her blessed. I realized one day that what is recorded about her is a synopsis of her entire life. She was probably not called "blessed" by her children until they were married and had families of their own.

There's something else we need to keep in mind. Her being called "blessed" was not just a result of what she had accomplished in life. It was the reward for who she was, for a total life lived in the fear and reverence of the Lord. What she *was* far outweighed what she *did*. She was busy, energetic, organized, and used her time wisely. But praise came because of what she was like while accomplishing those tasks.

> Strength and dignity are her clothing, and she smiles at the future. She opens her mouth in wisdom, and the teaching of kindness is on her tongue. . . . Charm is deceitful and beauty is vain, but a woman who fears the Lord, she shall be praised. (Prov. 31:25-26, 30)

The services a mother performs each day, such as changing diapers, washing clothes, cooking, cleaning, and caring for children, are relatively unimportant. Anyone can be hired to do them. What she *is* while performing those tasks, however, is critical. Anyone can replace the work a mother does. What can never be replaced is who and what she is while she is doing that work.

My children have never been overly concerned about the organization of our home. What they are interested in is the attitude and love Mom expresses. My teenagers watch how I react when four-year-old Danny needs comforting and I'm busy preparing supper. What am I like when they need to talk, and I'm frantically trying to keep on schedule? Do I become irritated by these interruptions or take the opportunities to give love and encouragement when needed?

WOMEN'S NEW FREEDOMS—AND FRUSTRATIONS

Recent years have seen the growth of the women's liberation movement. Women have "sprouted wings," encouraged to go far beyond diapers. Oriented more toward careers than "domestic living," they have become more aggressive. Women leaders have appeared in communities, rising up as powerful influences on many issues facing our nation.

Along with this new-found freedom comes frustration. So much is offered! Women, especially mothers, become overcommitted. Their time is torn between the needs of family and their own personal desire for "fulfillment." It is no longer considered "virtuous" to be a "stay-at-home mom," whose role is many times scorned by advocates of women's rights. Women find themselves in a transition, which brings tension, unrest, and strife.

Men have also been affected by these changes. Constant pressure to provide for his family "a better way of life" consumes his every thought and many of each day's hours. The ladder of success is available, and many are climbing with one thought in mind—attaining the "American dream."

But what is taking place on the home front? Mom is left with the responsibility of raising children without the support or presence of a father. The many long hours Dad puts in at work leave little time for interaction with his children. Time for maintaining a home, bathing children, helping with homework, relaxation, or just talking with them is at a premium.

Many husbands will encourage their wives to work in order to attain a higher standard of living or reduce financial stress. With this encouragement usually comes the promise to be more faithful in helping with domestic responsibilities. "Honey, if you go to work, we'll split the housework 50-50." It is a well-intentioned promise but not often fulfilled. After several months, Mom finds she has not only taken on employment outside the home, but has kept all the domestic responsibilities as well.

Statistics show that the average working woman will spend eight hours each day at work and one to two hours in travel time. Yet when she returns home, there's up to five hours of housework waiting for her. It is easy to see the problem many American women face in regards to time. There seems to be none of it left for the extras, especially relaxation! Single mothers have even greater demands on their busy lives. They need God's wisdom in abundance as they raise families alone, oftentimes under great financial stress.

Adding to her stress are children who are involved in sports, music, dance, gymnastics lessons, Girl Scouts, and Boy Scouts. You name it, and they are participating in it. This exposure is supposed to produce well-rounded children—but what about Mother? Her life becomes a whirlwind of activity filled with exhaustion. Well-rounded children are produced by a mother who is relaxed and enjoying life, not one who is frazzled and tired.

It is somewhat ironic that women of such a liberated society still find themselves imprisoned in so many ways. We are being made captives of time, with no apparent way out from behind its bars.

It is time to evaluate our lives. We have been duped into believing that the busier we become, the more fulfillment we will experience. We are spending our allotment of time on things that will not last forever. God's way is so contrary to our way. Isaiah says: "In repentance and *rest* you shall be saved, in *quietness* and trust is your strength" (30:15, italics added). The American way equates strength with activity and being saved with having enough material wealth to keep alive and well in this world. Our problem with time is the result of listening to the lies of the enemy rather than to the wisdom of God in His Word.

GOD'S PERFECT TIMING

Lying in the recovery room after delivering Daniel, I was left with my thoughts. At age 39 I was a mother to four teenagers, and now to a brand-new baby. After almost eight years of "freedom," I would now be returning to what I described in my book *A Mother's Touch* as the "desert years." The responsibility was overwhelming, and the lies of Satan began to come at me.

What am I going to do with a baby in my busy life? I thought. I knew a new baby in any home meant an automatic 40 percent increase in a mother's work. How would I be able to continue in the things I was doing—speaking, writing, and maintaining a household of four busy teenagers—and still remain sane? If it had been possible, a "pity-city convention" would have been held right there on the spot. Satan was trying to destroy the joy Warren and I had just experienced in giving birth to a beautiful, healthy baby boy. He was trying to convince me to look at Daniel as a burden, an inconvenience, instead of a blessing from God. I thank God for His great power at work within me that accomplishes exceeding abundantly beyond all I could ever ask or even think of (Eph. 3:20). I thank Him for allowing me to see this precious gift of a baby as His will for my life.

God's timing is always perfect. He knew in 1979 that my life would one day be full of busy teenagers, a husband whose ministry would be to thousands of people. He knew I would be called to be a writer, conference speaker, and mother of a baby. As a result of His foreknowledge, He prepared me. He taught me the many lessons I would need to learn in order to handle the life I now experience. Great is His faithfulness! I thank Him for His steadfast love and mercy which never ceases and is new to me each morning (Lam. 3:22-23).

Time will always be at a premium. Immediate needs will always be there, pressing for instant responses. In the following pages you will not be challenged to have the cleanest home or become the most involved woman in your church or community. You will not be called upon to be a "supermom." Learning to do the will of our Heavenly Father is the key to unlocking the secret of time. Through the life of Jesus, we will see that mystery of time begin to unfold.

Chapter 2

Help, I'm Drowning!

As I anxiously watched the young man in the department store climb up and down the ladder, I thought to myself, *Doesn't he know Christmas is still two months away? What in the world is he doing?* From his arms he was taking garlands of red and green tinsel and delicately draping them from the ceiling of the store. *Shouldn't someone tell him,* I thought, *not to be in such a rush to hurry the season?* He was not the only one promoting Christmas. It was only the first of November, but all around me were signs that "the season to be merry" was fast approaching.

The premature Christmas decorations set off an alarm in my brain reminding me of Christmases past. My memory brought back the anxieties that are so often a very real part of the traditional holiday preparations.

Most women, especially mothers, will be able to identify with the frustrations brought about by many American traditions surrounding Christmas. To already burdensome schedules is added more shopping, baking, and cooking. Housecleaning, decorating, entertaining, and activities at home, church, and community usually fill the month of December and leave little time for personal reflection. Sewing machines once again begin to hum with the making of gifts, little dresses, and costumes for the Sunday School nativity play. Somewhere around December 15 many mothers throw up their hands in despair. It dawns on them: "I'm never going to make it in time!"

Will mothers ever be able to sit back, relax, and wait for Christmas to happen? Will joy ever be the main ingredient in their preparations?

When the New Year comes, resolutions are made not just about Christmas but about life in general: "This year is going to be different. Spring cleaning *will* take place! I *will* clean my oven and refrigerator. I *will* redecorate my daughter's room as I promised, using that paint and wallpaper I bought three years ago. I *will* sort through all my pictures from the past five years and get them into albums. I *will* be more diligent in prayer and the study of God's Word." I will, I will, I will—the list goes on.

TIME TO BE A MOTHER

What a struggle mothers face in their pursuit for self-fulfillment as they find so little time left over after filling the demands children bring. They quickly realize that it takes an enormous amount of time and energy to be a good mother. In the midst of all their struggling is the desire placed in their hearts by God to be good at what they do. They want to be mothers who are in control of their situations, raising spiritually, emotionally, and physically sound children.

How blessed are the children whose mother takes time to recognize the important things when the urgent is constantly calling! In the midst of her busy day she takes time to be alone with her Lord, enjoying the refreshment which His presence brings. There is time for laughter, for creative play and teaching. The truly meaningful things of life are valued, and the superficial takes second place.

I often recall my own mother's ability to stop what she was doing to capture a memory. She had four very active children, two teenage sisters, and one teenage brother to care for—a total of seven children. Our home was always filled with activity.

Mom would keep us occupied during rainy days by emptying her cupboards of canned goods and allowing us to create our own grocery store in the living room. She never apologized to anyone for the mess we made. When a friend visited, Mom simply explained what fun her children were having.

Many times she would give each of us a stack of old blankets and allow us to build a "tent house." Furniture would be moved around and books were stacked in just the right places to securely fasten the blankets. What fun—but what a mess! After our little tent homes were built, our dolls settled in, and our tea sets and pillows properly in place, Mom would visit each of us and have her morning coffee break. Sometimes these organized, creative messes would last for days before we would tire of them.

Creating fun-filled memories in the midst of a time-pressured life is something that needs to be rekindled in our families. Playing house or store, having tea with doll babies, coloring pictures, making cookies, and being involved in creative projects have been replaced with either more intellectual or more passive activities. The TV and computer have too often replaced one-to-one interaction between parents and children.

As a young mother I desired my home to be filled with the love of Jesus; I wanted the noise and laughter of happy children to permeate the dust kicked up from children wrestling on the living room floor. Dishes in my sink were often a sign that I had decided to rock my two-year-old and read him a story or finally take time to paint a picture. An unmade bed in the afternoon would be the result of having four little ones snuggled up beside me, each with a book to read.

There is no question in my mind that one of the most treasured gifts a mother can give to her children is her time: to listen, to play, to laugh, and to love. God has not yet taught me the secret of having an immaculate home, "squeaky clean" and glistening to the eyes, but He has opened my eyes to the importance of order and using the time He has allotted to me for His glory.

TOO MANY ACTIVITIES

In 1979 it was apparent that I was in a maze of activity with four children fast approaching the frantic teen years. It was a critical time, a time filled with many urgent matters.

Involved would be the key word to describe my children's lives, and their activities so often became my activities. Field trips, class parties, and rides for kids to and from social and athletic events were part of my life. I used to think, *Don't these children know I have a house to clean or other things to get done?* I was frustrated, and I rebelled. Life was pressing in on me, leaving little if any room for quiet.

No longer did my life center only on my family. In my church I was appointed Director of Women's Ministries, which involved organizing retreats, conferences, and Bible studies for women. Then God opened doors to minister outside my church, speaking to women in a variety of church and denominational settings.

To coordinate schedules with my husband and children seemed impossible. I was running around in circles, and I felt a constant urgency. The thought kept going through my mind, *Is it all worth it?* I became so tired of trying to fulfill today's image of supermom. I was exhausted.

I wanted to withdraw from all activity. I knew I could throw up my hands in despair and quit. Quitting would have been a way out—an easy way out. It also would have been exactly what Satan would have desired. But I needed not only to recognize the problem, but to face it, asking for the wisdom of God. Certainly He was willing to teach me.

James says to "count it all joy" when you encounter all kinds of troubles. In *The Living Bible* it says:

Dear brothers, is your life full of difficulties and temptations? Then be happy, for when the way is rough, your patience has a chance to grow. So let it grow, and don't try to squirm out of your problems. For when your patience is finally in full bloom, then you will be ready for anything, strong in character, full and complete. If you want to know what God wants you to do, ask Him, and He will gladly tell you, for He is always ready to give a bountiful supply of wisdom to all who ask Him; He will not resent it. (James 1:2-5)

My life was most definitely full of difficulties and temptations. Trying to "squirm out" of my problem was not the answer. I was soon to learn the hard lesson of being ready for anything. The answer to my time problem would come as I sought God's wisdom.

I will instruct you and teach you in the way which you should go; I will counsel you with My eye upon you. Do not be as the horse or as the mule which have no understanding, whose trappings include bit and bridle to hold them in check, otherwise they will not come near to you. (Ps. 32:8-9)

DOES GOD CARE?

Part of me doubted: Could God really take this chaotic situation and bring about order? Was He even interested in my insignificant problems? One of those problems was my desperate need for a typewriter. Since many evening hours were spent away from home typing Bible study lessons at the church office, I came to a point where I said, "Lord, if You want me to continue in women's ministries, then You'll have to provide me with a typewriter." Of course my idea of God's provision would be an IBM Selectra.

Shortly after that prayer, a neighbor who was moving invited me and the children to sort through the many articles they would be disposing of before the move. As if in search of buried treasure, my children rummaged through the things earmarked for disposal.

On the garage floor in an obscure place I spotted a typewriter. At first I was hesitant to ask whether it was one of the items destined to go, but then I felt a boldness come over me. "Does this typewriter work?"

"It sure does," my neighbor said. "My wife has typed two papers for her master's degree on it. Would you like it?"

I couldn't believe what I was hearing. "Do you need another one?" came the second question. "There's one in the basement. It needs some clean-up and repair. Maybe your kids could use it."

I chuckled inside. These were not the IBM Selectras that I had had in mind, but I had asked for one typewriter, and here I had two of them. I was convinced that the Lord truly has a sense of humor. This typewriter was an answer to my prayer. It has since been replaced by a more efficient word processor, but it will always be a special reminder to me of God's love and provision. He *was* interested in my problems!

I was now ready to venture into discovering what the Lord required of my time. He knew the desires of my heart. Even more, He was ready to bring order out of chaos and ministry out of frustration.

TAKING JESUS' YOKE

What did the Bible have to say about time? As I was waiting for the children to get ready for church one Sunday morning, I thumbed through my Bible and began to read Matthew 11:28-30.

Come to Me, all who are weary and heavy-laden, and I will give you rest. *Take* My yoke upon you, and *learn* from Me, for I am gentle and humble in heart; and you shall find rest for your souls. For My yoke is easy, and My load is light. (Emphasis added.)

I had read that portion of Scripture many times, but that morning it took on new meaning. I quickly underlined and circled the three verbs: *come*, *take*, and *learn*. This was my answer.

Jesus knew of my weariness and the struggles I faced. He also knew that, from my heart, all I wanted was to serve Him as a good wife, mother, and servant in ministry to other women. His invitation was there; He awaited my response to it.

When my husband was ordained into the ministry, a beautiful, ornate stole was placed over his shoulders. It symbolized the yoke of ministry God had bestowed on him. Each Sunday he wears that stole as a reminder of his calling. Was I willing to take the Lord's yoke and to take it graciously, as a gift from His hand?

The yoke, I learned later, was designed for two oxen. It prevented the one from stepping ahead of the other as the fields were plowed. It caused them to work together in harmony, which made the task easier for both. If one kept rushing ahead of the other, if he was rebellious or wanted to do things his own way, he would become exhausted from fighting a losing battle. As he relaxed and rested, allowing the yoke to keep him in line, the work load was made lighter and the task was accomplished more efficiently.

Jesus had placed a yoke of ministry on my shoulders, the

ministry of serving my family and instructing women in the Word of God. So many times the desires of self or the pressures of the world would cause me, like the strong-willed ox, to jump ahead of Him. Work was getting done, but not efficiently, because of my unwillingness to be at the side of Jesus. With self in the lead, there was only conflict, and with conflict came resistance and wasted energy. No wonder I was exhausted!

I also learned that the farmer usually placed an inexperienced young ox in a yoke with a more mature, seasoned ox. The more knowledgeable one would restrain the younger from pulling ahead, teaching him how to work in harmony.

I was yoked with Jesus, the experienced teacher. He had become man and learned the secret of living for 33 years in the will of His Heavenly Father. He promised to be gentle and lowly of heart in His teaching. When I jumped ahead, He was ready to discipline me and encourage me to stay at His side. I was in the process of being trained. As I learned from Jesus, the yoke of ministry grew more easy and the burden I carried more light.

ORDER FROM STILLNESS

My anxiety caused me to continually jump ahead of God's plan. He had appointed a time schedule for me. Solomon says it so wisely: "There is an appointed time for everything. And there is a time for every event under heaven" (Ecc. 3:1). Verse 11 of Ecclesiastes 3 reads in the *Amplified Bible*: "He has made everything beautiful in its time."

I am the type of person who wants everything done yesterday. In my mind I planned each move toward restoring order to my frenzied life. The big "I" always wanted to pull ahead of Jesus' plan. I lacked patience and trust. Jesus had an appointed time for order to begin, but the foundation had to be laid if it was going to be of any lasting value.

The call from the Lord was to learn and to be still before Him. "Cease striving and know that I am God" (Ps. 46:10). I was to let go and relax in the presence of the Lord. In my letting go of self I would come to really know Him as the sovereign Lord of my time.

My human nature rebelled; because I was such an active person, I found very few moments where I was content just to sit still. My life had become so cluttered with activity that there was little time for enjoying His presence. It was not that I didn't read my Bible and pray. I was faithful in that area of my devotional life, but it was always on the run and mostly out of a sense of duty. It was just another religious activity that took up time. God was requiring something new: quietness, stillness. He longed for my attention. He wanted me to listen to His gentle voice. His desire was for me to experience a love relationship, an intimate knowledge of who He was.

I knew this would take time. Other things would have to wait. At times I would rebel because humanly speaking it did not make sense. There was so much that needed to be done; urgent tasks were calling me. Matthew 6:33 kept coming to mind: "But seek first His kingdom and His righteousness; and all these things shall be added to you." Unmade beds and dirty dishes would have to wait. My time with the Lord was of prime importance. I longed to become reacquainted with my "first love." From this relationship would spring an ordered life lived for His glory alone.

LIVING FLEXIBLY

During those times of quiet before the Lord, I began to realize how resistant I was to change. With the passing of time, my needs and the needs of my family had changed. I was no longer the mother of four preschoolers. My circumstances were different, but I subconsciously insisted that my schedule must stay the same.

After Daniel was born I struggled for greater flexibility. I was 39 years old and my life was very structured; I had goals that I was determined to reach. A baby was not going to hinder me. I tried desperately to keep life going as it had before, but Danny would not comply to my schedule. As an infant, he had needs which far outweighed my need for cleaning house on Fridays or washing clothes on Monday. I resisted changes, and tension began to build. It wasn't until I let go and began to relax that peace was restored.

Schedules during the baby, toddler, and preschool years revolve around meals and naps. The need for Mom to be home is usually more crucial, so she tends to accomplish quite a bit of housework and domestic chores.

As the children enter elementary school, changes begin to take place. These years become some of the most freeing years in a mother's life. With the last little one in school, Mom begins to venture out into the world. She may consider part-time or full-time employment. At the same time, she gets involved in her children's school and learns the meaning of the term *car pool*. Where her schedule once revolved around domestic responsibilities, it is now regulated by the number of activities her children participate in. She encounters a new problem, as it gets harder to get things done at home.

The teen years arrive all too quickly. Physical exhaustion is now teamed with emotional weariness. During the teen years a mother is usually experiencing hormonal changes. Dealing with her own mood swings is difficult enough, but now she also has to deal with the hormonal changes taking place in her teenagers.

Both need understanding and love. They need to spend time with one another, but Mom finds herself emotionally drained. Physical fatigue results from the energy expended in emotionally charged situations. Work and schedules get put aside, and she is forced to deal with the emotional aspects of raising children.

Once again she needs to be flexible in her scheduling. Ross

HELP, I'M DROWNING!

Campbell in his book *How to Really Love Your Teenager* (Victor Books) says that teenagers need more time with parents than do toddlers. They need you there, but on their terms. They are the ones who determine when quality time will take place. We like to think we can arrange for these times, only to find that our teens aren't necessarily ready to interact when we are.

This chapter began with a description of the panic many mothers experience during the holidays. As I am writing these words, Christmas is just three weeks away. It is one of the busiest times in our family. Will there be tense moments? Undoubtedly, yes! But celebrating Christmas now is altogether different than it was back in 1979.

At the beginning of the Advent season each year I ask God to bless our family's Christmas preparation. I desire to have my heart prepared for Christ's coming more than anything else. I want the joy of Jesus to permeate all the activities. Some things won't get done on time. I ask the Lord for wisdom to help me distinguish between really essential things and those that only consume my time.

What special event are you preparing for? Is it a birthday party for one of your children, a confirmation, graduation, or anniversary? There are always deadlines to meet and promises to keep. How are you handling these pressures? Do you feel as though you are drowning in a sea of activity? Jesus says to you, "Come unto Me . . . Take My yoke upon you, and learn from Me."

Chapter 3

Busyness

It was a frantic Friday in the Arndt household. Any outsider observing Warren and me that morning would have thought we were plotting out battle tactics.

With pen and paper in hand, Warren began to map out our strategy for the day. The problem before us required some planning: all four of our teenagers were to be involved in different activities, three basketball games and one volleyball game, all in different places, at approximately the same time. How could two parents get four children to places miles apart on time?

Warren shook his head and laughed, "Elise, if we had only known fifteen years ago what we know know, maybe we would have done things differently!"

One afternoon I was placed in charge of driving Liz, John, and their friends to and from their games. Seven hours later I looked at the speedometer and found I had driven close to 100 miles in one afternoon and evening.

There were times when I questioned whether what I was doing was good stewardship of my time. *Am I being fair to myself?* I asked myself. At times I felt imprisoned in my car with teenagers who were either pouty and quiet or so full of energy that they wouldn't shut up. What a challenge! Certainly my time was too valuable for this. Surely I could have been doing something more constructive than driving all over Detroit and the surrounding suburbs.

Very often while waiting or driving, I would diligently make a mental checklist of the many things I could have been doing. A spotlessly clean house, supper on time, the laundry folded, and my schedule of getting things accomplished were all put aside for this time in my children's lives. Driving, waiting, sharing, and being with them was what the present demanded.

IS BUSYNESS WRONG?
I used to feel extremely guilty if I got too busy. I had to come to grips with what I was doing and seek guidance from God's Word and not from human wisdom.

Busyness is not essentially wrong. Frustration comes when our busyness is not profitable. Jesus may have been the busiest person who ever walked the earth. John 21:25 records, "And there are also many other things which Jesus did, which if they were written in detail, I suppose that even the world itself would not contain the books which were written." We need to evaluate the content of our busyness.

We mothers need to examine our busy lives. We need to go to the Word of God for direction. We need to examine the busy life of Jesus to get clues to survival in these years of seemingly unending activities.

As I began to examine those years of being so busy with my children, I saw the value of the many hours I spent driving them to and from various places. In my car, I had a captive audience. Certainly there were times when they didn't want to talk. It was difficult for me to sit in silence, but I learned to be patient and not take their silence as a personal affront to my motherhood. At other times I couldn't keep them quiet. They were chatterboxes, filled with exciting news of the day.

I especially enjoyed carpooling when the car was filled with their friends. I learned much about what was taking place in their lives just by listening to them talk. They seemed to forget I was there behind the wheel. Many times I would have to restrain myself from laughter, other times from shock.

Car pools, sometimes called the curse of motherhood, became blessings in disguise, for in those endless hours of driving I got to know my children. Maybe it was because we were not looking eyeball to eyeball. We shared a sense of freedom, a relaxed attitude. Talk would often center on their many insecurities about boy-girl relationships, teachers, homework, and their relationships with God.

It was a busy time in my life, but worth every moment. It was a time I will always remember as being an investment in their lives.

BUSY AT WORK

One of the best things any person can do is to be busy and to work hard. Work was created to be a blessing, not a curse. It is a gift to us from God. Anyone who has been sick or otherwise unable to work knows what I mean.

Here is what I have seen to be good and fitting: to eat, to drink and enjoy oneself in all one's labor in which he toils under the sun during the few years of his life which God has given him; for this is his reward. Furthermore, as for every man to whom God has given riches and wealth, He has also empowered him to eat from them and to receive his reward and rejoice in his labor; this is the gift of God. (Ecc. 5:18-19)

Each summer I enjoy canning and freezing fruits and vegetables. It is tedious, time-consuming work, but I enjoy what it produces. Last summer I canned 36 quarts of tomatoes. I was so proud of my accomplishment! With the jars filled, I was anxious for some recognition. Instead of quickly putting them away, I purposely left them on my kitchen counter. I was sure my family would proclaim that I fit the description of the virtuous woman of Proverbs 31. Even though my back ached and my hands looked like prunes, I felt good about myself. My day was profitable. I had accomplished something.

Maybe you have the same feeling after cleaning the house, washing windows, or doing a good deed for someone. There is something to be said about hard work and being busy. It gives a person a sense of well-being, of self-worth. I believe that as we learn to set goals and accomplish them it will build self-esteem, especially when the work involves pleasing others.

JESUS THE TIME MANAGER

I want so much to be like Jesus. He was the perfect time manager. From Him we can learn how to deal with busyness. From Him we can learn what is profitable and what should be eliminated.

What was Jesus' secret to having a life of order and accomplishing the task for which He was sent? Did He have 36 hours in His day instead of our 24? Was He physically stronger than we are? Was He able to go without sleep? It says in the Bible that He worked from sunrise to sunset, but nowhere does it say He worked through the night. He had a human body, like ours, which required sleep and food.

Hebrews 2:17-18 gives me comfort and encouragement.

Therefore, He had to be made like His brethren in all things, that He might become a merciful and faithful High Priest in things pertaining to God. . . . For since He Himself was tempted in that which He has suffered, He is

39

able to come to the aid of those who are tempted.

Jesus was made like us in all things. He too struggled with time pressures. In reading the first eight chapters of the Gospel of Mark, we find Jesus constantly pressured by people and their problems. He was tempted to react as we do. I am sure He became tired and frazzled. I am sure there were times in His humanity when He was tempted to waste time or to be busy doing things that would not have been profitable. With crowds pressing in on Him, Jesus would leave a situation and escape to the wilderness, mountains, or the sea in an effort to get away and be in communion with His Heavenly Father. He knows what we are experiencing and has promised to come to our aid.

In my study of the life of Jesus and time management, I found several themes that revealed to me the secret of His productive, fruitful life in the midst of busyness.

SURRENDERED TO GOD

Jesus' public ministry began with an act of obedience, His baptism (Mark 1:9). He humbled Himself and did the will of His Father. The result was the anointing of the Holy Spirit and the pronouncement from the Father, "This is My beloved Son!" He was empowered for ministry. Jesus gives to us the example of obedience. He demonstrates time and again what it means to have a submissive will.

As we begin this venture of learning to invest our time wisely, we must be willing to submit to and obey our Heavenly Father. Unless we surrender our selfish wills and lay aside what our human natures want, there will be no divine reproduction of the life of Jesus within us. It is only when we humbly submit in obedience to God's will that the blessings of a well-ordered life begin to unfold and we begin to witness productivity.

Our obedience will be tested as Jesus' obedience was. Mark records that Jesus was impelled by the Spirit to go into the wilderness to be tempted by Satan for 40 days and nights (Mark 1:12). Only three temptations are recorded in Matthew 4:1-11 and Luke 4:1-13, but the original Greek states that He was *continually* tempted by Satan. I believe every temptation imaginable was thrown at Him during this time; yet He resisted and was found without sin.

We also are going to be tempted. When a person sets out to do the will of God, Satan will put up a fuss. What a comfort to know we have a God who understands our problems and has gone before us so that we can claim victory!

A PURPOSE FOR LIVING

Another main ingredient in the life of Jesus was that He knew why He had been sent to this earth. He had a purpose for His life. Luke 19:10 states, "For the Son of Man has come to seek and to save that which was lost." After just three short years of His public ministry Jesus was able to declare, "I glorified Thee on the earth, having accomplished the work which Thou hast given Me to do" (John 17:4). Jesus had clearly defined goals. All of His energy, His busyness, centered on this one goal.

We also need to have goals in our lives. Lack of clearly defined goals wastes time and energy. Without goals, we wander aimlessly, with little or no purpose. Goals give a purpose to living and doing.

THE REQUIREMENT OF REST

From Scripture we learn another secret of how Jesus was able to accomplish so much in His short lifetime. Rest and relaxation were part of His busy life. How easy it is to forget that Jesus had a frail body like ours! He too required food and rest. Many times He felt the need for periods of personal refreshment away from His work and people. We find Him in the Gospel accounts frequently withdrawing to be alone (Mark 1:35; 2:13; 3:7; 4:35-36; 6:30-31).

Mark 6:31-32 tells us that Jesus planned vacations with His disciples. "And He said to them, 'Come away by yourselves to a lonely place and rest a while.' (For there were many people coming and going, and they did not even have time to eat.) And they went away in the boat to a lonely place by themselves." Jesus knew when His disciples had had enough. He did not wait until things slowed down. People in need were all around Him; yet He took out time to withdraw.

Many Christians are in the process of burning out. They are exhausted because they have not learned the secret of relaxation in the midst of busyness.

God's intent for humankind was a balanced life of work and relaxation. He sets the example in His creation of the world. Six days He worked and on the seventh day He rested. Our life should follow the same principle: 6/7 work and 1/7 rest. It is God's plan for us.

The fourth commandment seems to have been revised to accommodate modern life. Instead of "Remember the Sabbath Day, to keep it holy," many would like it to read, "Remember the Sabbath Day, to keep it busy." Sunday is no longer considered a day of rest. For many women, it is a catch-up day. Housework, shopping, or the myriads of things that didn't get done during the week get done on Sunday. Stress—one of the major causes of health problems in the United States—is the price many are paying for not learning to relax as God intended.

My husband and I have established a precedent (maybe even a tradition) for our family. Sunday afternoons have been set aside as relaxation time. We try to keep this time free from any type of activity that would take us away from home. I have broken our earlier tradition of preparing a big meal after church, because it involved too much time and effort. Sunday's menu now consists of simple dishes like soup and sandwiches. There have been exceptions, but generally we are very protective of this day of rest. We need it. It is a day for worshiping the Lord and renewing our bodies as well as our souls and spirits for the coming week.

Daily we need to take time to relax. My mother, an extremely wise and practical woman, encouraged me as a young mother to set aside time each day to rest. "Don't feel guilty about taking naps when your children do. Housework can wait. Your children need a rested, happy Mom more than they need a clean house," she would say.

As my children became older and resisted their naps, I still insisted that they go to their rooms to read or play for just one hour. They did not have to sleep, but they did have to be quiet. Often I would set a timer for one hour of quiet. I needed the time of separation and quiet for myself. It prepared me for the coming evening.

Scheduling quiet time in your busy day should not be an option; it should be a requirement for a productive life as a mother. Don't feel guilty in the midst of busyness to take time for yourself. You need it!

THE URGENT AND THE IMPORTANT

Another one of the lessons Jesus teaches us about time management is to accomplish the important things when the urgent is calling. He had His priorities in their proper order.

The urgent matters of life are those that demand our immediate response, the things that constantly bid for our attention. They give no consideration to what is presently being done. They include annoying interruptions at the wrong time for the wrong reason and the pressing needs of people around us. These are the urgent matters of life.

While the urgent continually begs for our attention, the important keeps silent. It patiently waits for us to take notice. While the urgent seeks us, the important waits to be sought by us. The important aspects of life take discipline to perform, while the urgent are accomplished on impulse.

Extra time with the children in creative play and projects, letters of encouragement, prayer, Bible study, visiting a sick neighbor or friend, making that needed phone call, starting that diet, and taking time to relax can all get put aside when the urgent calls.

Jesus was often plagued by the urgent. He easily could have been distracted from the important things He was doing, but because He had a goal, He wasn't distracted.

In Mark 5:22-43 we find Jesus, on His way to an important task, being interrupted by an urgent matter. Jairus, one of the synagogue officials, comes to Him and asks if He would heal his daughter, who is at the point of death. Jesus, filled with compassion for the man, starts to go with him to his house. But on the way He is interrupted by a woman with an "issue of blood." Does He ignore the urgent matter? No, He gives in to the moment, acknowledges her, and ministers to her. In the excitement, Jesus could easily have forgotten His original goal of going to the house of Jairus. He could have stopped and preached a sermon on the qualities of this woman's faith. He didn't; He had an important matter to attend to.

I wonder what Jairus was thinking. Quietly observing the Master, He probably wanted to hurry Jesus along, but he patiently waited. Then the news came to him: his daughter had just died. He must have been filled not only with sorrow, but also with anger and resentment. Jesus understood and turned to Jairus in the midst of all the excitement about the woman's healing, and said, "Do not be afraid any longer, only believe" (Mark 5:36).

Jesus had a goal, the goal of healing Jairus' daughter. He was not going to allow the urgent to deter Him from accomplishing the important.

We live in constant tension between the two, don't we? Filling the needs of the moment causes us to become weary.

We blame hard work for our anxiety. In reality, it is not hard work that produces stress, but doubts and misgivings about what we are doing. We have become slaves to the urgent.

Our problem goes much deeper than just a shortage of time. Our priorities are jumbled. When we allow the important to take precedent over the urgent, our stress is relieved.

How did Jesus tell the difference between the urgent and important? "He Himself would often slip away to the wilderness and pray" (Luke 5:16). He prayerfully waited for His Father's instructions. He discerned the Father's will—what was important—daily.

How do you start out your day? Are you so busy doing your own thing that you do not have time to listen to the still small voice of God directing your day? The Word of God tells us, "Seek ye first the kingdom of God, and His righteousness; and all these things shall be added unto you" (Matt. 6:33, kjv). We need times of quiet before the Lord as we begin our hectic days. Establishing a quiet time actually saves time!

WISE INVESTMENT OF TIME

Jesus also knew the secret of where to invest His time. To invest it unwisely is wasteful and leads to "time poverty." From the Scripture we see that He didn't invest time in the abundance of things (Matt. 8:20). He did not even have a place to lay His head. He invested in the lives of people and in communion with His Heavenly Father.

The world's philosophy is "Invest your life in the *things* of this world. Build for this present life." Scripture clearly warns us against placing great value on material possessions. Luke 12:15-34 tells us that our lives are not made up of the things we own.

What is the most important thing in your life at this moment? Is it your home, financial security, status, job? If it is not your relationship with Jesus, you could be wasting a lot of precious time. Only two things are going to last forever: people and the Word of God. All else will eventually be destroyed. I want to make an investment of my time, as Jesus did, in things that are of eternal value. Peter wrote, "All flesh is like grass, and all its glory like the flower of grass. The grass withers, and the flower falls off, but the Word of the Lord abides forever" (1 Peter 1:24-25). According to 1 John 2:17, people are also going to last forever. "And the world is passing away, and also its lusts; but the one who does the will of God abides forever."

When we die, we will not be able to take one material possession with us, yet many of us live as if we are trying to build kingdoms on this earth. We absorb material possessions as a sponge soaks up water. We need to be admonished as Martha was: "Martha, Martha, you are worried and bothered about so many things; but only a few things are necessary, really only one, for Mary has chosen the good part, which shall not be taken away from her" (Luke 10:41-42).

Paul, my oldest son, was sometimes a clumsy teenager. He was growing so fast that his body seemed to get places before he did. On my dinette wall is a beautiful curio cabinet. In it are all of my little treasures, things that have been given to me by special people. One particular treasure was a delicate china cup and saucer that Warren's grandmother had given to me for Elisabeth. It was a genuine antique, and I loved it. One day Paul entered the dinette area, and his shoulder hit the edge of the curio cabinet. *Crash!* Everything was on the floor. Elisabeth's cup and saucer were broken into pieces. My first reaction was anger. "Can't you be more careful? How can you be so clumsy?" Then I saw the downcast look on his face. He hadn't intentionally caused the accident. Immediately I was convicted. I had placed more value on a thing than I had on a young boy's life and emotions. I picked up the broken pieces, held them in my hands, and with tears in my eyes told Paul how sorry I was for reacting the way I had. And then, I said something that eased the pain in my heart over the loss of my treasured cup and saucer. "Paul," I said, "this cup and saucer are not going to go with me into heaven, but you are. I'm sorry I placed more value on it than I did on you."

In what are you investing your time? We all need to come to grips with this question. Until we examine our lives in this area, the time we spend is likely to be unprofitable, bearing little fruit.

Do you consider yourself a busy person? The only way to discern if your busyness is wrong is to seek God's will. If you are desirous of doing what God wants you to do, He will help you come to understand the difference between the urgent and the important. All He requires is an open heart that desires to obey. The frustrations of time pressures will always be there; there is no escape. But frustrations will not overwhelm us when we know that our busyness is subject to His will.

Chapter 4

Discipline for the Long Haul

My clothes were beginning to feel snug, but with the polyester clothes that were so popular in the 70s, an extra few pounds could always be squeezed in. It was soon apparent, however, that the material was being stretched to its capacity, and that dieting was in store for Elise Arndt. How I fought having to lose weight!

I described my struggle to a friend. It's always interesting to hear another person's solution to your problem. My friend, Dot, felt my answer would come through a new Christian diet program. Since she also had to lose a few pounds, Dot suggested that we lead the program together.

The last thing I wanted was to get involved in teaching another Bible class. "Don't you know how busy I am, Dot? I just cannot commit to another thing." I tried to stand firm with my excuses, but somehow she convinced me to at least give it a try.

As I examined the materials, I realized I was in deeper than I had anticipated. Along with learning to eat properly and exercise, the program included a challenge to be disciplined in our spiritual lives as well. Dot and I agreed to be under each other's authority. If we were going to teach others, we had to be examples for them. I have to admit that I rebelled many times against her supervision. I didn't like the idea of someone monitoring my behavior: what I ate each day, my exercise, my devotional life. I felt as though I was in a battle—my way against God's way, my will against His.

My struggle with dieting was only a reflection of a much deeper problem. God was working. He was teaching me what it means to be a long-distance runner, not just a sprinter, in the Christian life. I was learning how to submit to God's authority, to present myself as a "living sacrifice" before Him (Rom. 12:1-2), and that was totally opposite what my human nature wanted. It was an uncomfortable feeling, and I resisted.

CHAOS REIGNED

Since my return to the United States in 1972, I had become very undisciplined. I was taking care of such things as laundry, general housekeeping, and meal preparation at bare minimum. I spent more and more time away from home involved in many activities. So I had little time to do the necessary tasks to keep our household running smoothly. I constantly allowed urgent matters to dominate my lifestyle. I put off answering letters, writing notes to teachers, making phone calls, and finding baby-sitters until the last minute. I misplaced children's homework assignments, mail, receipts, and other important papers on a daily basis.

I tried to remember everything, but too often I missed appointments. Once as part of a car pool, I showed up at the wrong place at the wrong time. I couldn't understand how other people managed to stay on schedule.

I had asked God to discipline my life and bring order into my chaotic situation. Now this diet program appeared. Could this be God's way of answering my prayer for a more organized life? One of the key verses that I learned during the weeks that followed was Hebrews 12:11: "All discipline for the moment seems not to be joyful, but sorrowful. Yet to those who have been trained by it, afterwards it yields the peaceful fruit of righteousness." It was a difficult 36 weeks. Submitting to several sets of disciplines and being accountable to someone was a true source of agony for me. It violated what my human nature wanted. The only thing that kept me going was the promise of Hebrews 12:11. How I needed peace! I knew it could only be given by the author of peace—Jesus Christ Himself.

PEACE TAKES THE THRONE

Evidence of this peace began to show itself in my daily schedule. I began to see results. Spending time alone with God in a disciplined way provided me with a stability throughout my day. I had a new strength welling up inside me that helped me resist the temptations of not only food, but also procrastination, and giving in to the urgent when the important was waiting. I was learning to yield to God's authority and trust Him that the peace would be there. The lessons I learned did not come easy, but they were long lasting in what they produced—"the peaceful fruit of righteousness."

As I began to set goals and seek ways of accomplishing them, something began to happen. That year, when Christmas appeared, I was actually ready for it! How I used to envy people who had their Christmas cards ready to be mailed the day after Thanksgiving. Now *I* was the one in the post office buying stamps and proudly depositing my addressed cards in the mailbox. I put up the decorations weeks in advance. I completed my daughter's dress, and had it hanging in the closet ready for her to wear. That in itself was a major accomplishment, since I had become convinced that sewing on Christmas Eve was an inevitable part of the harried Christmas tradition. There was no last-minute purchasing of Christmas gifts. The presents were wrapped and placed under the tree ahead of time. That year I actually sat and waited for Christmas to happen.

Other changes began to appear in the Arndt household: clothing actually made it to dresser drawers from the laundry table. My husband marveled at the ironed shirts in his closet and socks and underwear in his drawers. Files began to appear, the checkbook was balanced, the children's lunch money was ready the night before, a calendar appeared by the phone, and a little black notebook accompanied me everywhere. My life began to take on order. The first people who noticed were the members of my own family; they could sense I was a happier person. Sometimes I would revert back to my old ways, which they referred to as my "crazy lady routine." But now more often than not my life exhibited calmness; serenity; an attitude of control. I was at peace.

I became organized in spite of the fact that my pace was still escalating. My calendar became filled with speaking engagements and other types of ministry to women in other churches. I still had a long way to go, but I was on the right track. The "peaceful fruit of righteousness" was beginning to show. In my desire to be obedient to the Lord, I was being blessed.

THE BLESSINGS OF OBEDIENCE

In Deuteronomy 28, that great chapter on the blessings of obedience, Moses stands before the Children of Israel and charges them to keep the commandments of the Lord so that when they enter the Promised Land they will receive the blessings God had promised them.

> Now it shall be, if you will diligently obey the Lord your God, being careful to do all His commandments which I command you today, the Lord your God will set you high above all the nations of the earth. And all these blessings shall come upon you and overtake you, if you will obey the Lord your God. (Deut. 28:1-2)

Later Moses warns them about the effects of disobedience.

> But it shall come about, if you will not obey the Lord your
> God, to observe to do all His commandments and His
> statutes which I charge you today, that all these curses
> shall come upon you and overtake you. (Deut. 28:15)

Obedience to God always produces blessings, while disobedience produces curses. It is as simple as that. In order to
experience a life of joy we need to be obedient.

The writer of Hebrews tells us to fix our eyes on Jesus,

> who for the joy set before Him endured the cross, despis-
> ing the shame, and has sat down at the right hand of the
> throne of God. For consider Him who has endured such
> hostility by sinners against Himself, so that you may not
> grow weary and lose heart. You have not yet resisted to
> the point of shedding blood in your striving against sin.
> (Heb. 12:2-4)

Jesus looked forward to joy in the midst of His agony. He
knew what the final outcome would be as He sacrificed Himself
upon the cross for our sins. He was willing to experience pain
because of what it would accomplish. In being obedient to the
will of His Heavenly Father, He found joy.

Because Jesus had a human nature as well as a divine nature,
He had to learn obedience. He was given a task to do: to seek
and to save a lost, dying world and to draw all men unto
Himself. In order for this to be accomplished, He had to put
aside what His human nature wanted and do only the will of
His Heavenly Father. That took discipline. He struggled just as
we do. Hebrews 5:8-9 records:

Although He was a Son, He learned obedience from the

things which He suffered; and having been made perfect, He became to all those who obey Him the source of eternal salvation.

His obedience took Him all the way to the cross. It is important that we understand this about Jesus. He also had to learn obedience. What comfort to know He has gone before us and endured every struggle we will ever have to encounter. And He was victorious!

Just before Jesus was to die for the sins of the world, He went to the Garden of Gethsemane to pray. He knew what was ahead of Him. He knew the suffering and pain He would soon be enduring and He asked His Father if there was another way.

He . . . fell to the ground, and began praying that if it were possible, the hour might pass Him by. And He was saying, "Abba! Father! All things are possible for Thee; remove this cup from Me; yet not what I will, but what Thou wilt." (Mark 14:35-36)

Jesus was in total submission to His Heavenly Father. Our human natures tell us to rule our own lives. Jesus shows us through this act of obedience that only when we let go of what self wants can the divine will of God be manifested. Obedience is the true mark of the disciple and one of the ways of experiencing the "abundant life" Jesus has promised.

FLESH VERSUS SPIRIT

Our spirits are willing for the life of obedience and the discipling of God, because the Holy Spirit within us prompts us toward what God wants. Then why doesn't it take place? Paul in Romans 7:18-23 explains:

For I know that nothing good dwells in me, that is, in my

flesh; for the wishing is present in me, but the doing of the good is not. For the good that I wish, I do not do; but I practice the very evil that I do not wish. But if I am doing the very thing I do not wish, I am no longer the one doing it, but sin which dwells in me. I find then the principle that evil is present in me, the one who wishes to do good. For I joyfully concur with the law of God in the inner man, but I see a different law in the members of my body, waging war against the law of my mind, and making me a prisoner of the law of sin which is in my members.

There is a constant battle being waged within the life of every believer—the battle between flesh and spirit. It is easy to know what we should be doing, but putting it into practice is another thing. God's desire for us is to have every area of our lives brought under the control of the Holy Spirit so that we might glorify Jesus Christ. He is willing to accomplish this. Putting knowledge into action is what discipline is all about.

Hebrews 12 is a great chapter on the discipline of the Lord. We need to read this chapter often as a reminder of what God wants from us.

It is for discipline that you endure; God deals with you as with sons; for what son is there whom his father does not discipline? But if you are without discipline, of which all have become partakers, then you are illegitimate children and not sons. Furthermore, we had earthly fathers to discipline us, and we respected them; shall we not much rather be subject to the Father of spirits, and live? For they disciplined us for a short time as seemed best to them, but He disciplines us for our good, that we may share His holiness. (Heb. 12:7-10)

God's discipline is always for a reason. The Children of Israel

roamed in the wilderness for 40 years. They continually dis-
obeyed God, and the results were lives full of misery. He wanted
them to enter the Promised Land as a purified people who had
learned obedience. Through discipline He prepared them.

Are you wandering in a desert? My desert was a disorganized
life that was unprofitable and filled with frustration. I was
disobedient to the Lord in what He wanted to accomplish in
me. I wanted to do things my own way. Until I learned to
submit to what He desired, I couldn't enjoy the pleasures of the
Promised Land.

Discipline's purpose is not to make people into robots. God
does not violate our free will. He always gives us a choice in
matters relating to daily living. Discipline's purpose is to produce godliness: "that we may share His holiness." It is designed
to bring order into chaotic lives; to build self-control, and to
make us into a godly people so that "we might proclaim the
excellencies of Him who has called [us] out of darkness into His
marvelous light" (1 Peter 2:9). God's love is continually manifested to us through the disciplining process.

Our sinful nature rebels against discipline. We want everything to come easy. We cringe from change because it causes
pain.

The word *discipline* means "work," sustained daily effort.
The word Paul used for discipline is the one from which we get
our English words *gymnastics* and *gymnasium*. Dictionaries
state that discipline is a branch of knowledge or learning. It is
also described as training that develops self-control, character,
orderliness, and efficiency.

Only after many years of subjecting his or her body to hard
work and practice does an athlete become successful. That
continual daily effort is an essential part of the conditioning
that prepares the athlete for competition.

And everyone who competes in the games exercises self-control in all things. They then do it to receive a perishable wreath, but we an imperishable. Therefore I run in such a way, as not without aim; but I box in such a way, as not beating the air; but I buffet my body and make it my slave, lest possibly, after I have preached to others, I myself should be disqualified. (1 Cor. 9:25-27)

Continued daily effort is an essential element of Christian discipline. Jesus said, "If anyone wishes to come after Me, let him deny himself, and take up his cross daily and follow Me" (Luke 9:23). What does it mean to take up one's cross and follow Jesus? I used to think it meant bearing an illness or some type of trial. The true meaning of taking up one's cross is really the denial of self, the death of self, putting aside the desires of the natural man. It means putting aside what self wants and doing what God wants.

The denial of self will be painful. It was for Jesus in the Garden of Gethsemane. He struggled with His humanity; we will too. As God shows you certain attitudes, feelings, and habits that need to be laid aside, new God-directed ways will replace them. He will show you, if you are open, your habits of housekeeping, devotional life, relationships, and other habits that have been keeping you from moving on. A simple thing like rising 15 minutes earlier in order to start out your day with the Lord will be difficult. Resisting the urge to watch TV or read that favorite magazine or newspaper when there is work to be done will be painful. Putting aside whatever has been keeping you from getting things accomplished will cause rebellious feelings to well up inside.

POWER TO WIN

This battle of the flesh against the spirit can only be won through the power of the Holy Spirit operating in us. We must recognize that. Although we are very weak—really incapable of winning—Jesus is strong and has fought the battle for us. "Therefore I am well content with weaknesses, with insults, with distresses, with persecutions, with difficulties, for Christ's sake; for when I am weak, then I am strong" (2 Cor. 12:10).

It is God who works within us. When we recognize we have no place to go and no one else to turn to; when we see the inability of our human nature to even want to desire the things of God, and how the sin in our lives separates us from enjoying the blessings of God, we become convicted of our dependency on Him alone. We must declare with Peter, "Lord, to whom shall we go? You have words of eternal life" (John 6:68).

Maybe you are up against a wall with no where to go. You have tried everything you know with little success. It's time to try Jesus' way. He will take you step by step.

CHOOSING SELF-DISCIPLINE

Our wills are involved in the adventure of discipline. So many times we wait for the right feeling or for a direct revelation from God, a bolt of lightning to get us motivated. Many Christians never get past the feeling level of their faith. Living controlled only by their weaknesses, they experience failure and end by giving up. We need to be patient. We will fail at times, but we must allow God to forgive our shortcomings. The Holy Spirit will pick us up and give us a new start. God's Word promises that: "For I am confident of this very thing, that He who began a good work in you will perfect it until the day of Christ Jesus" (Phil. 1:6). The only time discipline fails is when we give up.

God doesn't violate our freedom of choice. We can choose to do things God's way, which leads to blessing, or do it our way. God will do His part in causing us to desire His will and give us the power to accomplish it, but we must do our part and *act*. We need to come to God at the point of our need and trust that He will direct our paths (Ps. 37:5).

MARATHON DISCIPLESHIP

We need endurance. Think of how easy it would have been for Jesus to give up. He came to a world that rejected Him, yet He persevered. He continued because He knew what the outcome would be.

Enthusiasm is great, but sustained daily effort is what we need. The excitement of getting started will soon wear off. I became excited about the possibility of writing another book, but when the realization came that it was going to take a daily commitment—a daily sacrifice of my time and self—I began to have second thoughts. The thought of having a house in order is exciting, but having to do a little each day to see that it is accomplished soon turns into drudgery. It doesn't seem very glamorous in the nitty-gritty of each day.

God has given us a marvelous capacity for forming habits. A habit is something we do at a semiconscious, automatic level. Habits come into our lives as a result of discipline. Some of the basic time-management habits that we may need to change have to do with meeting deadlines, finishing tasks before moving on to others, and taking care of ourselves through proper diet and exercise. When we practice discipline in areas of our lives on a daily basis, we form habits. We establish ways of doing things without thinking much about them. It may be a real chore to make your bed every morning, but if you do it consistently, it will become a habit.

Remember when you were a child, and you were first learning to ride a bike or roller-skate? You fell often in the training process, and it hurt, but you stayed with it until you learned. You endured in spite of your many failures. The disciplining of our lives will be hard work. Many times it will be painful, but what it will produce is a lifestyle that will bring glory to God.

In a world that promotes doing your own thing, we have little desire for discipline. A structured way of life is made to appear too restricting. Yet those who have sought disciplined lives have found the opposite to be true. Discipline brings freedom.

I am often reminded of this as a parent. My children are the happiest when they know what is expected of them. When they know the boundaries, they feel free. I love the example Jay Adams gives in his little booklet *Godliness Through Discipline* (Presbyterian and Reformed Publishing Co., p. 13). "When is a train most free? Is it when it goes bouncing across the field off the track? No, it is free only when it is confined (if you will) to the track. Then it runs smoothly and efficiently. It needs to be on the track, structured by the track to run properly."

Structure is necessary for our lives too. We need to be on track, and that track is the Law God has given us in His Word. When we operate according to our Maker's specifications, contentment, peace, and order will be the result.

WHERE DO I START?

Are you undisciplined? Is your life in a state of confusion? Are urgent matters keeping you from accomplishing what is important? Maybe you have never been faced with developing discipline in your life. You ask, "How do I start? What should I do?"

First, you must recognize that the problem is not your circumstances or another person; it is you. You need to change in your heart first. You need to be willing to accept responsibility for the chaos around you and confess before God your lack of discipline and unwillingness to do what He wants.

Once we accept His forgiveness, we can go on to the next step, acknowledging His desire and ability to work within us. He can and will change us. He will reveal His will for our lives. He is not a God of confusion; He desires order in your life. He has a plan and purpose for you. Before you were born He knew each one of your days (Ps. 139:16). He created you with a purpose—to glorify God (1 Cor. 6:20, 10:31). God plans good for your life, not evil (Jer. 29:11). He does not will any evil to come your way. His purpose is to give abundant life (John 10:10).

We must recognize that we are powerless to change on our own. All discipline should be motivated by the Holy Spirit. Daily, we need the filling of God's Spirit. He is our motivator. He is our power source. Daily, we need to ask for His help. In our quest for becoming more disciplined, we must seek God above all else.

I find that the busier I get, the more time I need to spend with God. He is my source of strength and direction. His Word guides me in my endeavors. I need those quiet times alone with Him every day.

We may have all the spiritual principles and knowledge of discipline, but nothing happens until we do something about it. Paul in Philippians 3:12-14 writes,

Not that I have already obtained it, or have already become perfect, but I press on in order that I may lay hold of that for which also I was laid hold of by Christ Jesus. Brethren, I do not regard myself as having laid hold of it yet; but one thing I do: forgetting what lies behind and reaching forward to what lies ahead, I press on toward the goal for the prize of the upward call of God in Christ Jesus.

We too are to press on. The entire process of discipline requires persistence, endurance, sustained daily effort.

Paul had a single-mindedness about him: "one thing I do." How many times do we allow distractions to prevent us from finishing a project? Goal setting will help us keep on track.

We must also learn to forget what lies behind and reach forward to what lies ahead. We cannot be buried in the past or use it to excuse our behavior. God forgives our past mistakes and each day gives us a new start.

Today is a new beginning for you and me. No matter what kind of mess we are in, we can have a new start. Our efforts may not make much difference at the beginning and we may not see quick results, but they will come. Maybe you will only accomplish one thing, but you will have accomplished something. You will be encouraged to go on. You will feel good about yourself.

An exciting adventure lies ahead of you. Allow the Lord to show you the areas in your life that need changing. Confess these areas to Him and desire change. Then do what He requires of you. Don't expect it to come easy. The disciplined life will cost you something, but in the end, you will be overwhelmed with what God will work in your life.

May our Lord Jesus give you strength to endure and may you rest in His love and the assurance that His strength is made perfect in our weakness.

Chapter 5

My New Friend—
My Notebook

P sychologists say that we retain only 10 percent of what we hear and less than that if something else of greater importance distracts us. When I heard that, I began to understand something about myself. Something of greater importance was already crowding out what I was supposed to remember. Approaching middle age was not the cause of my loss of memory; I was just an average person with an average memory. Committing to memory all the appointments, schedules, and activities of the other six members of my family seemed to be an impossible task. I had an average brain with an average capacity to recall only 10 percent of what I heard. No wonder I was having a hard time!

People's important and urgent needs surrounded me. The immediate concerns of my family and the needs of my extended family of church and community were all pressing in on me. I made promises to remember people in prayer with the best intentions, but they were soon forgotten. Committing to memory the days I was responsible for a car pool resulted in children calling from school in desperation. "Mom, where are you?

We're waiting for a ride home! You were supposed to pick us up!"

WRITE IT DOWN

I knew the answer for remembering was writing things down. The less you have to keep in your head, the clearer your mind is for productive thinking. Somewhere I read an old Chinese proverb: "The palest ink is stronger than the strongest memory." "Off my mind and onto paper" began to be my slogan. Writing everything down freed my brain from the worry of forgetting. It was a great idea but not without its problems. Those little slips of paper with their important messages, telephone numbers, appointment times, and prayer requests were hard to find. They found their way to one of three filing places: my purse, my Bible, or the kitchen counter.

When I opened my Bible to search for a note, papers would fall and scatter on the ground. I had to empty my purse in futile attempts to find that needed date, address, or telephone number. My kitchen counter grew cluttered with school papers, mail, newspaper articles, Bible study papers, and various other important items.

Writing things down had alleviated the worry of forgetting, but now I had a new problem—trying to find what I had written down. Disorganization was my middle name, and it robbed me of precious time.

MY SERIOUS PROFESSION

There had to be a better way! My husband has always been an extremely organized and efficient person. Efficiency and promptness are natural to him. Seldom did he miss an appointment or forget to answer a letter. Later I found out that Warren used time-management techniques in his profession. His datebook accompanied him everywhere. He consulted it often to make sure he was on the right track. He depended on it so much that without it he would be lost. It irritated me; I was jealous of the "love affair" between him and that little book, and I often threatened to hide it.

Why didn't some of these organizational skills rub off on me? Perhaps I didn't look at my role of homemaker seriously enough. Yet I believed it was a profession, a calling that required as much organization as any large corporation.

My confusion was not part of God's plan for our home. I read 1 Corinthians 14:40: "But let all things be done properly and in an orderly manner." I do not believe Paul wrote those words only for the church in Corinth. They were words that could be applied to Elise Arndt and every other mother in regard to her home.

Stephanie Winston, author of *Getting Organized* (Warner Books) has counseled many people on ways to impose order on their everyday lives. "What they have in common," she says, "is that they all perceive themselves as victims of paper interruptions and their inability to make many small decisions. They feel overwhelmed." Her definition of being organized is "being able to find what you want when you want to find it and accomplishing what you want when you want to accomplish it" (*Weight Watchers*, November 1980).

I wanted my home to be filed from A to Z. It was not so important that it be immaculate; all I needed was to be able to put my finger on things and not waste precious time in search of lost articles. On the other hand, I wanted a balance that allowed for necessary interruptions. Babies do cry, the telephone does ring, and emergencies do occur. I had to be able to cope with the unexpected. Those moments of stopping the clock to make a memory were important. Taking time to listen to a child explain his point of view, to admire God's beautiful creation, to listen to the heartaches or joys of a friend—these were all necessary. I aimed to have a general plan or structure to my day, but surprises like these were to be treated as special incidents rather than interruptions.

My teacher in this adventure of organization had to be the Creator of time. I asked God for His help, and I believed the answers I sought would be found in Him.

A LITTLE BLACK BOOK

I decided to take action. I thought of a notebook like the one my husband used. If it worked for him, it could certainly do the same for me. For less than $5 I became the proud owner of a small, black notebook. Not a bad investment for something that has lasted for almost eight years and has saved me countless hours of looking for lost information!

I have been asked many times, "Why a notebook?" I'm sure there are many other ways of recording information. A home computer, a calendar near the phone, and a filing cabinet are some. But none of these is as portable as my notebook. How many times in the course of a day do you need to find a telephone number, grocery list, receipt for the cleaners or shoe repair, clothing sizes, dimensions of a window, or directions to someone's house? If you are far from home, a filing cabinet or computer is of little use. A notebook can be small enough to fit in your purse.

I have fallen in love with my notebook. It has become a dear friend that accompanies me just about everywhere. Like my husband, I too would be lost without my notebook. I have found it so satisfying that I have developed two notebooks, one for all the data needed to manage my home and the other for spiritual management of my life. That second one stays next to my Bible. In it is information about my daily walk with Jesus.

Beginning a notebook will take discipline. I have just learned how to operate a word processor. There were many times when I thought it would be easier to go back to my typewriter. I felt safe and secure in my old ways and fearful and intimidated by this strange-looking machine, which required perseverance and a new way of thinking. It has been well worth the effort. To begin something new is always a challenge, but in the end you are much further ahead.

Your notebook will be a type of computer. At first it will take work to enter all the information. You may even say as I did, "I don't have time to organize a notebook." But once done, you will wonder how you existed for so many years without it.

GETTING STARTED
All that you need to get started is a small loose-leaf notebook, a pack of loose-leaf paper to fit, section dividers with plastic tabs (I could not find any at first and had to make my own dividers), and a pocket calendar, with squares big enough to write in.

Work on only one section of your notebook at a time. The divided sections should be suited to your needs. Each person is unique, so don't feel confined to the directions I give.

The three sections that will probably be the most beneficial in starting are your Bible study section, your "Things to Do" section, and your calendar.

Other sections might include ones for your family, diet and menu planning, finances, and clubs and committees which you belong to. There is no end to the sections you can develop to meet your needs.

THE BIBLE STUDY SECTION
First let's take a look at the section designated for Bible study. Later as your notebook develops, you may want to have this section in your spiritual notebook, but for now, it can be in this one notebook. Developing your "spiritual notebook" will be discussed in another chapter.

Time-management principles for the Christian begin with Matthew 6:33: "Seek ye first the kingdom of God and His righteousness and all these things shall be added unto you"

(KJV). In our quest for managing our time and getting the most out of each day we must remember that God comes first. I would suggest writing out Matthew 6:33 on the top of your title page in your Bible study section of your notebook as a reminder that your relationship with the Lord and the study of His Word is of prime importance. Once we understand and practice that principle, everything else will fall into place.

In the Bible study section you will want to record three things on a daily basis: the date, the portion of Scripture you have read, and what you have learned (practical application).

As you are reading God's Word a particular verse may jump out at you. Underline it in your Bible, and then write it on one of your pages. This exercise will help implant the verse on your mind. Then, write what it means for your life, in your present situation. Reflect and meditate on these words during the day.

It is only after you have spent time alone with the Lord in the study of the Word and prayer that you will be ready to move on to the next section of your notebook, preparing your list of things to do.

THINGS TO DO

Your list of things to do will be a result of communing with God in prayer each day. Quite often, while in prayer, thoughts come into my mind that are totally unrelated to what I am praying for. I may be praying, "Lord, please be with Sue," and the thought of defrosting the hamburger for supper or sending a card for my nephew's birthday comes into my mind. I used to be troubled when that would happen; I felt my prayer time should not be interrupted. What I have learned to do is stop my praying and write those thoughts down immediately on my things-to-do list. Once it is on paper, it is off my mind, and I am free to continue with my prayer time. Give in to those interruptions at the moment; they may be God's way of ordering your day. "The steps of a man are established by the Lord"

(Ps. 37:23). I always keep my notebook close by during my quiet time with the Lord just for this purpose.

Your "things to do" section will contain what you would like to accomplish in the coming day. List all the many tasks that need to be completed: errands, telephone calls, letter writing, birthday and anniversary cards to be sent, your grocery list, and so on. As you make out your list, you will find that you are writing down the *important* matters of life. Writing down the important helps ward off the urgent!

It has been estimated that only 25 percent to 50 percent of a manager's time is spent according to self-chosen plans. For this reason, I schedule only half of my day. This allows for unexpected interruptions and alleviates frustration in trying to cope with the stress that comes with the urgent matters of life. I plan on the urgent being there daily. If I allot time for these unplanned interruptions, I feel more at ease with myself. If the unexpected doesn't appear, then I have extra time to allow me to do something for myself.

Many of us make lists, but time management experts say that we miss the next essential step—setting priorities. We need to ask the questions, What should I do first? What can be done only at certain times? What can I omit altogether?

When you list "things to do" according to priorities, you are making choices. Susan Reeve, a therapist and organizational consultant who helps businesses and individuals get their time priorities in order, has this to say: "It is not so much doing things more efficiently, but making choices about what you want to do that makes you feel better about yourself. When you just do whatever comes up, you've already made a choice—that of no choice" (*Parent's Magazine*, November 1981).

Your list of things to do will be challenging. You will at times receive great satisfaction as you make it out and then proceed to scratch things off as they are accomplished. What a good feeling! But there will be other times when you feel the list is endless, and nothing seems to be getting done. Each new day brings with it a carryover from the previous day's list. Remember on those days that if you have accomplished only one thing, and it was the most important item—the one at the top of your list—your day has been successful.

"Don't allow list making to steal your joy or spontaneity. The whole point of managing your time," says Robbie Fanning, author of *Get It All Done and Still Be Human*, "is to remove the pain so you can get on with living, not to propel you into compulsive non-stop activity" (*Parent's Magazine*, November 1981, p. 86). There will always be more you could be doing. Each one of our lists could be endless, and it is easy to become overwhelmed with all that needs to be done.

Keep in mind that your schedule is your slave. Don't allow your list to control your every move. When you become a slave to your schedule, you are missing out on what God desires for your life. Be open to changes. You are going to experience "slump days," days on which you feel like doing very little. Go out to lunch, take a walk with a friend, enjoy life. It takes an intelligent woman to realize she is not superwoman. Jesus rested in the midst of great urgency. He withdrew even though the multitudes were pressing in around Him. Your list is just a helper, a friend, designed to make life easier, to free your mind from clutter and allow you to think more positively and clearly about life.

YOUR CALENDAR

The fun part begins when you begin to write on your calendar the many activities of each week. When you call for a dentist appointment, write the time in the appropriate date space. Indicate your car-pool week with an arrow going through the number of days you have to drive. Two days before someone's birthday write, "Buy card—send to Mom."

One of my projects on New Year's Day is making out my

calendar for the coming year. I list every speaking engagement, each one of my children's activities, everyone's birthday and anniversary, our vacation time, and all doctor and dentist appointments. Then as other engagements come up, I know where and how to schedule them. I can also tell, at a glance, if I will be overcommitting myself. It makes it easier for me to say yes or no.

At the beginning of each week, I check my calendar. I am then able to plan meals accordingly. No roast beef dinner on a day which is filled to capacity with running errands! I can line up baby-sitters in advance rather than wait until the last minute. I organize the car schedule accordingly—in a family with six drivers, I have to arrange to have the car ahead of time. Each one of my children's activities is there for me to see and plan for. One clever mother suggested I use a different color pen to write each child's schedule. At a glance I could tell who was to be where and when.

My husband and I also coordinate our schedules. Twice each year, in the fall and in January, he inserts on his calendar pages every one of my speaking engagements. He knows what is before me each month. It has helped him understand when I need more support from him and the children. There has also been less confusion and conflict as we plan our schedules together.

One particular morning I became so engrossed with painting a room in our house that I forgot to consult my calendar. At 9 o'clock the phone rang. It was Warren. "What are you doing home?" he said in astonishment. "You are supposed to be in such-and-such a place." I had completely forgotten my appointment. I thank God for my dear husband who consults his calendar daily and prays accordingly for me. That morning he called home to see how our son was managing with the painting. My voice at the other end of the phone totally shocked him. I believe God directed him; his call saved me from total embarrassment at not showing up at an important meeting. It taught Warren and me to check on each other and coordinate our schedules. It also gives us the opportunity to pray for one another specifically as we realize what each is facing each day.

SCHEDULING HINTS

Make your calendar work for you. Fill in the spaces with scheduled activities. Here are a few ideas that may help you in scheduling.

• Learn to bunch activities. Have one day to run your errands: grocery shopping, banking, dry cleaners, post office, hardware store, etc. Plan beforehand the most timesaving route to go. By bunching activities, you will be able to do more in less time.

• Reduce decision making by scheduling specific jobs for specific days. Maybe we should think about going back to the "old-fashioned" pattern of washing on Mondays, ironing (does anyone iron anymore?) on Tuesday, cleaning on Fridays, etc. I have found getting back into a routine of doing things on certain days has helped me to reduce the number of decisions I need to make, and the result has been less tension. I have a specific goal for each day.

• Learn to divide large jobs; don't try to do it all in one day. If you are thinking about redecorating a room in your home, begin by scheduling a time to choose paint color. Make a list of all the needed items and spend another day purchasing them. Schedule one day to move furniture and patch any holes in the wall. Finally, schedule a day where you do nothing but paint, even if it is only one wall each day. In one week you could have the room completed. Segmenting jobs helps you set realistic goals.

• Avoid unnecessary distractions. When you work, turn the TV off. If it is on, it will distract you from your scheduled activity. Something will catch your eye, and before you know it, you will be sitting down to watch. I also don't answer my telephone on days of heavy-duty work, or I have someone else answer and promise that I'll return the call later. Answering machines are wonderful for this purpose.

● Set time limits. Set a goal for yourself in a specific time frame. When that job is completed, reward yourself with a ten-minute break. Fix yourself a cup of coffee or nice cool drink. Before starting another job, take out time just for yourself. It sure breaks up the routine.

● Avoid being negative. There is always so much more you could be doing. Decide what you are going to do, do it, and forget about what you haven't done. If it is scheduled, you will handle it in its turn. If it's not scheduled, it probably isn't important enough to be done at all.

● Learn to say no nicely. One of the most valuable skills I've learned lately is that of saying no. Just by looking at my calendar I am able to tell when I can accept an engagement and when I cannot. I have learned to schedule cautiously, and it has relieved the feeling of guilt I used to experience when I said no.

Are you excited about the possibility of getting organized? There is hope for anyone. Developing your notebook can be a great blessing in your life. Be patient with yourself. Give God time, but on the other hand be obedient to His will for your life. Take one step at a time. The situation you are in did not develop overnight. The solution will take a little time. Old habits will need changing. It may take days or weeks to undo a bad habit and replace it with a good one. Be persistent, and most of all, "trust in the Lord with all your heart, and do not lean on your own understanding. In all your ways acknowledge Him, and He will make your paths straight" (Prov. 3:5-6).

Chapter 6

Without a Vision, a Mother Perishes

The countdown had begun. Only three more weeks and our third child, Elisabeth, would graduate from high school. A party was being planned, graduation announcements and invitations were sent, and a dress had to be bought. Great excitement and anticipation filled our home as we prepared for this major event.

My children stood at a distance and observed their mother's "crazy lady routine" once again. They shook their heads as I tore apart closets and cupboards, washed curtains, and cleaned all those hard-to-get-at corners of the house. John shook his head when he found me cleaning the track of our sliding door with a toothbrush. It was the most ridiculous thing he had ever seen.

"Why are you getting so fanatical?" was his question.

My children usually just smile and shake their heads at my crazy antics until I insist they become involved. Since I have three strong boys, I take advantage of their strength and ability to wash walls, paint, and do general heavy-duty work. I use every free moment they have to get them involved. "Who

73

cares?" is their reply when I con them into working. "Why work for weeks painting, cleaning, and moving things around for a party that will last only five hours?" To the average male— especially young boys who would rather be doing other things—all this fuss is absolutely inessential.

MOTIVATED BY A GOAL

Isn't it strange how a simple thing like a party can act to spur us on to accomplish things that have needed to be done for years? When a goal is before us, we buckle down. Even such a simple thing as inviting the neighborhood women over for a morning coffee can send some women into a frenzy of cleaning. Places ordinarily left untouched get cleaned. Warren contends we need one celebration each year just to motivate us to get things done.

Isn't human nature funny? Instead of learning to pace our daily activities, we wait until we feel pressured to get things done. Do you realize that God knows this about us? He understands that without a vision or goal we will never reach our full potential. A goal causes us to form a mental picture of what can take place, so we spring into action; we become motivated to actually do something outside our present routine. It is difficult to work toward something if you don't know what that something is.

Studies have shown that top achievers have three major characteristics in common: they have a mission to which they are dedicated; they set short-term, realistic goals; and they have positive expectations.

Ask any mother of the bride how she plans the many details of her daughter's wedding months in advance. She becomes dedicated to a mission; she sets realistic goals, and has positive expectations. Is it not realistic to assume that the everyday tasks of life can be dealt with in a similar manner?

One of the fundamentals of time management is setting

goals, and one of the major requirements for living a productive Christian life is having a vision. Proverbs 29:18 clearly states: "Where there is no vision, the people perish" (KJV). Peter Marshall said, "Too often we aim at nothing and succeed in hitting it." Alan Lakein, in 1976 the president of the only company in America devoted exclusively to time-management, said this:

> Most people don't think in terms of minutes. They waste all the minutes. Nor do they think in terms of their whole life. They operate in the mini-range of hours and days. So they start over again every week, and spend another chunk unrelated to their lifetime goals. They are doing a random walk through life, moving without getting anywhere. (Quoted by Jane O'Reilly in "How to Get Control of Your Time (and Your Life)" *New York Magazine*, January 17, 1972)

When I was first challenged to set goals, it seemed impossible. How could I set a target for my life when I struggled every day with what to prepare for supper? I was too preoccupied with the moment to be concerned about what my life would be like tomorrow, much less one year from now or beyond.

TOO MANY CHOICES!

Why all this talk today about goal setting? Is it really all that important for women to have clear-cut goals? In the past such a topic would not even be addressed. Women often had fixed schedules. It was a life dictated greatly by routine and primarily centered on home and family.

What a difference a couple of decades can make! The woman of today's society is bombarded by choices from both inside and outside her home. With every situation, she encounters a decision. Choices surround her, and she is free to pick and choose. But whenever choices are multiplied, frustrations become multiplied.

The years we lived in New Guinea taught us how simple life can really be. Simplicity was the result of having very few choices. Monday and Thursday were always wash days, Tuesday was baking day, and Friday was the day our wood stove and kerosene refrigerator were cleaned. Wednesdays I made arrangements for cargo carriers to go to the airstrip and pick up our supplies and mail for the week. Mealtimes and our daily contact with the mission via two-way radio at scheduled intervals throughout the day kept the routine going. Bedtime came early each night. Since I had no access to grocery stores, all my shopping was done through the mail, which eliminated agonizing decision making. Sometimes we liked what we got and sometimes we didn't, but we couldn't complain because we had no choices.

Arriving in the United States brought real problems in the matter of choices. Walking into a supermarket made my head spin. The many choices available to us in our society demand that we set goals that can help us focus our decision making and save precious time and energy.

In order for your home to operate smoothly, there needs to be order, routine, and a general plan and structure to your life. You need to know where you are going and what steps are needed to get there. Goal setting helps us make decisions. When you establish a goal, you can channel your energy into making decisions to meet that goal. You become single-minded.

I often wonder what it would be like to take a long trip in a car without a map. Precious time would be wasted as you encounter detours and snags. Having to stop at numerous gas stations to get directions would cause unrest to spring up among your passengers.

The same thing happens with our travels in life if we wander aimlessly, never taking the time to plan. When we get lost along the way, we become irritated and our frustrations are shared by others.

Before we go any further in talking about goal setting, one principle must be clarified for the Christian. Everything we do should be in submission to the will of the Father. John 5:30 gives us the example of Jesus: "I do not seek My own will, but the will of Him who sent Me." Our Heavenly Father must be in charge of our goal setting. James reminds us of this:

> Yet you do not know what your life will be like tomorrow. You are just a vapor that appears for a little while and then vanishes away. Instead, you ought to say, "If the Lord wills, we shall live and also do this or that." (James 4:14-15)

I constantly need to be reminded to submit to God's will for my life and not stubbornly demand to do things my own way. It is so important to seek the Lord and ask for His direction.

WHERE TO BEGIN

A good plan for setting goals does not begin with a list of duties, but with an evaluation of what your life is all about—your personal values. Without personal goals in mind, you may spend time and energy on projects that are not important to you. There are four types of personal goals: lifetime goals, professional goals, short-term goals, and weekly or daily goals. Woven in these four areas are your spiritual, emotional, personal, and family goals.

The most difficult part is starting, but taking the first step is the most important. When you start writing down your goals, try to form a mental picture in your mind of what the accomplished goal will look like. Picture a room free of clutter or a slimmer you. Picture yourself as an author or student. If your goal is to save for a vacation, find a picture of that longed-for vacation spot and put it in a place you can see.

No matter how foolish your goals may seem, write them down. You are not telling God anything new; He knows the secret desires of your heart. If they are wrong desires, and if you are open to doing His will, He will change them and give you even better ones. He says in His Word He will give us the desires of our hearts as we delight in Him (Ps. 37:4).

FIVE-YEAR GOALS

If lifetime goals seem too difficult to imagine, try to envision what your life will be like in the next five years. Maybe you will be free to go back to school and get that degree you always wanted. What about your husband? Are you looking ahead to the future together, to being able to spend more time together? What about your family and children? College plans? What are your goals in being a mother?

ONE-YEAR GOALS

If you cannot think in terms of lifetime goals or even five-year goals, think about next year. What would you like to accomplish in your home? In your spiritual life? Would you like to read through the Bible in the coming year? Have a more dedicated prayer life? Join a Bible study group? Establish a quiet time with the Lord? In your relationship with others, what areas need improvement? What about serving the Lord? Is there a ministry in which you would like to become involved?

What are your professional goals? If you aren't working outside the home, is there something you would like to venture into after the children are in school full time? If you are in the work force, do you want to improve yourself by getting specialized training? Maybe you desire a promotion or an increase in salary. Are there things you can write down to help you reach these goals?

Short-term goals are just as important to establish and write out. A goal of yours may be to lose five pounds within the next month or so. Or you may want to start a physical fitness program, redecorate a certain room, or be more diligent in reading to your children.

WEEKLY GOALS

If you find it hard to look even that far in advance, weekly and daily goals are always a must. Are there extra tasks you want to add to your schedule in the next few days? Some examples of these goals could be baking a birthday cake for a friend or child, giving yourself a perm, or starting a particular craft.

I hope by now you have purchased a little notebook as I suggested in chapter 5. In this notebook you may devote an entire section to your goals. You may want to write out James 4:15 or some other Bible verse on the divider page to help you remember that God is the one who directs your life.

It will probably take you several days to think of and write out your goals. You will probably have to revise them periodically. List them in order of importance in each of the categories. You won't be able to accomplish everything, so you need to decide which goals are most important to you. By knowing what your goals are, you will be able to evaluate the importance of your tasks.

KNOW YOUR WORK STYLE

Writing out goals is one thing, but doing them is another. You need to know your own distinct work style. Some people can handle one job at a time and do it well. When it is done, they go on to another. Others need several concurrent challenges to keep them from getting bored.

The fear of never having a big enough chunk of time to accomplish a job prevents many people from starting. Learning how to segment jobs and move toward goals ten minutes at a

time can help. Here is a list of things that can be done in just ten minutes.
- Clean a bathroom sink
- Exercise
- Write one thank-you note
- Set the table
- Plan one meal
- Feed a pet
- Water plants
- Read a chapter in the Bible
- Make a telephone call
- Do a load of wash
- Fold a load of laundry
- Read a story to your toddler
- Make a bed

KNOW YOUR TIME CLOCK

Get to know your own time clock. Some people fight their natural time clocks because they have developed schedules they assume cannot be changed. Determining if you are a lark or an owl—a morning person or an evening person—saves you valuable time.

When I am writing or doing any type of research, my peak time for concentration and creative thinking is in the early morning. Working at 5:30 A.M. gives me quality time in a house that will later bustle with the activity of a four-year-old and four older children. I discipline myself to rise early and make use of that quiet. I save routine work such as housecleaning, errands, shopping, and the laundry for late morning and early afternoon.

The woman who constantly fights her natural time clock forces herself out of bed early each morning even though she does not function well until 10 o'clock in the morning, and then only after three cups of strong, black coffee and a shower.

This same woman at the end of the day feels energetic and restless as she watches TV in the evening or cannot get to bed much before midnight. She needs to understand her peak times for work. It is not a law that housework must be done between the hours of 8 A.M. and noon. If you are most alert in the afternoon or evening, don't feel guilty about doing the bulk of your work at that time.

SLUMPS

A third thing to remember is that there will be times when you will experience slumps. On these off days we feel little direction or enthusiasm for doing anything. Because of the complexity of our physical and hormonal makeup, these days occur in every woman's life. We can learn to anticipate them and plan accordingly.

During certain times in a woman's menstrual cycle, she is a bundle of energy. There is nothing she can't do. This is when she decides to clean closets, wash windows and walls, go on a diet, or get to that project that has been waiting for months. Then for some unexplainable reason she becomes irritable, tired, sluggish, and unmotivated. Little gets accomplished during this time and what does get done is only that which she forces herself to do.

Much research has been done in the area of how a woman's menstrual cycle relates to her peak performance times. Our hormones are often responsible for the way we feel about ourselves and our energy levels. Dr. James Dobson, in his book *Straight Talk to Men and Their Wives* (Word Books), writes,

It has been said, quite accurately, that the four weeks of the menstrual cycle are characteristic of the four seasons of the year. The first week after a period can be termed the springtime of the physiological calendar. New estrogens (female hormones) are released each day and a woman's body begins to rebound from the recent winter.

The second week represents the summertime of the cycle, when the living is easy. A woman during this phase has more self-confidence than during any other phase of the month. It is a time of maximum energy, enthusiasm, amiability, and self-esteem. Estrogen levels account for much of this optimism, reaching a peak during mid-cycle when ovulation occurs. The relationship between husband and wife is typically at its best during these days of summer, when sexual desire (and the potential for pregnancy) are paramount.

But alas, the fall must surely follow summer. Estrogen levels steadily dwindle as the woman's body prepares itself for another period of menstruation. A second hormone, called progesterone, is released, which reduces the effect of estrogen and initiates the symptoms of premenstrual tension. It is a bleak phase of the month. Self-esteem deteriorates day by day, bringing depression and pessimism with it. A bloated and sluggish feeling often produces not only discomfort but also the belief that "I am ugly." Irritability and aggression become increasingly evident as the week progresses, reaching a climax immediately prior to menstruation.

Then come the winter and the period of the menstrual flow. . . . Gradually, the siege passes and the refreshing newness of springtime returns. (p. 163)

Have you noticed this about yourself? Are there times when you feel energetic and enthusiastic about starting new things? You feel good about yourself. Then, for no apparent reason, a dark cloud hangs over you. Everything seems overwhelming and impossible. Waiting a few days usually does the trick; soon you are back to your old self again.

Dr. Dobson stresses that self-awareness is the key to self-acceptance. When we understand our bodies, we can begin to work in harmony with them and not against them.

Get to know when your peak periods occur during the month. A calendar is all you really need. Chart your moods: Mark in red the days you feel good about yourself, the days of high energy levels. Mark in black or some other color the days of low self-esteem and sluggishness. Mark the days of menstruation and ovulation. I know you will be amazed as you see a pattern develop.

Charting has helped me understand why I feel the way I do at certain times during the month. I no longer plan big dinner parties or invite people over when I know I will be going through a difficult slump time. I use my high energy days to their fullest and try to accomplish as much as possible during them. On my off days I take on a lighter activity load and find things to do that can help me through that time. Lunch with a friend (which I don't seem to have time for when I am at a high energy level and cleaning like crazy) and extra telephone calling and letter writing help reduce the pressure and stress of having to accomplish a lot.

We all know that regardless of the way we feel, things still need to be done, and there are times when we must perform tasks even when we don't feel like it. Children do have birthdays, mothers-in-law do visit, and children graduate from high school during premenstrual tension times. Life does not always coordinate with your schedule. But just knowing what is going on inside helps me get through those times.

Lizzy graduated last week. We celebrated and had a party, which turned out beautifully. She is our only daughter, and I wanted it to be special. Everything was in order. I had a goal to attain, and all my energy was focused on reaching it. The house looks nice with its new wallpaper and curtains, and I'm so proud. We worked together with one goal in mind and it paid off—just a little example of what goal setting can do.

Chapter 7

First Things First

In God's work of creation, there is order. He created the millions of planets and their galaxies to exist in peaceful splendor. The Master Architect positioned the earth just the right distance from the sun, so that it would neither burn up nor freeze. His order for the seasons and His design of the human body exemplify such harmony in creation. Can you imagine what our world would be like without organization? Chaos would prevail, ending in destruction.

Just as God has called His world to exist in order, so He has purposed that those whom He has created live in order. When we rebel against that order, we choose a lifestyle of chaos.

When we allow God's design for order to control our lives, we exchange confusion for tranquility and peace. Instead of doing what others expect, we seek to do the Father's will, saving ourselves frustration, wasted time, and energy.

In God's design for His people, He comes first (Matt. 6:33). Then come our families and whatever work or ministry we carry on outside the home. Living successfully in the Christian life is in part a matter of priorities. When the fulfillment of self and what self wants becomes number one, we are in deep trouble. The decisions we make, how we react to situations, and how we deal with other people will be self-centered. James tells us the consequences of accepting the wisdom of self. "For where jealousy and selfish ambition exist, there is disorder and every evil thing" (James 3:16).

LOOKING OUT FOR NUMBER ONE?

The world reinforces selfish thinking. Every day we hear: "Do your own thing. Become your own person. You have your rights—fight for them. Don't let anyone push you around. Stand up for yourself."

God's Word instructs us: "Or do you not know . . . that you are not your own? For you have been bought with a price: therefore glorify God in your body" (1 Cor. 6:19-20). Jesus instructs us to

- deny ourselves (Matt. 16:24; Mark 8:34; Luke 9:23)
- put ourselves last instead of first (Matt. 19:30; 20:16)
- be meek (Matt. 5:5)
- be humble and not exalted (Luke 14:11; 18:14)
- become servants to be great (Matt. 20:26; Mark 10:43)
- be willing to die in order to live (John 12:24-25)

What a list of paradoxes! The priorities in a Christian's life follow a set of rules in opposition to our human natures. Jesus wants us to understand that His way is the only way to live and experience abundant life. God is a God of order! He expects our priorities to come under His divine system of order, not ours.

The first priority for any Christian is to love God above everything else: "Love the Lord your God with all your heart, and with all your soul, and with all your mind. This is the great and foremost commandment" (Matt. 22:37).

Loving God above everything else is where it all begins. If you love your profession, possessions, family, your humanitarian efforts to the world more than God, your life will be empty, void of meaning and purpose. You will be satisfying the desires of your flesh, living only for the present.

Nowhere is it more difficult to live out the Christian life than in our homes. Time and again we get in the way and try to prove that we have a better plan for raising our children than God. We feel we have the right to yell, scream, and nag because of our situations, never realizing that Jesus always gives us an alternative.

Being a mother means being a servant. But who wants to hear about servanthood today? In order for us to be effective in our mothering and in our Christian lives, we need a servant heart, which places others before ourselves. It doesn't come easily. Self raises up its ugly head and says no, I want to be served; I want to be acknowledged; I want to be pleased and recognized.

CRUCIFIED WITH CHRIST

If self is to die, the believer must be crucified. Paul describes it this way in Galatians 2:20:

> I have been crucified with Christ; and it is no longer I who live, but Christ lives in me; and the life which I now live in the flesh I live by faith in the Son of God, who loved me, and delivered Himself up for me.

The crucifixion and death of self involves four steps: separation, suffering, death, and finally resurrection. *Separation* from sin takes place once we become conscious of known sin. When that occurs you can be sure that the Holy Spirit is at work.

With the recognition of sin and the accompanying desire to separate ourselves from it, beware, for the next step will surely follow—*suffering*. Giving up sin in our lives is an agonizing process. Satan has made sinning to be enjoyable. To give up what we enjoy is never easy.

François de Salignac de La Mothe Fénelon, the Archbishop of Cambrai, France during the seventeenth century, penned many letters which have been translated into a modern paraphrased book, *Let Go* (Whitaker House). In this little book on what it means to die to self, Fénelon writes,

Whatever spiritual knowledge or feelings we may have, they are all a delusion if they do not lead us to the real and constant practice of dying to self. And it is true that we do not die without suffering. Nor is it possible to be considered truly dead while there is any part of us which is yet alive. This spiritual death (which is really a blessing in disguise) is undeniably painful. It cuts "swift and deep into our innermost thoughts and desires with all their parts, exposing us for what we really are." The great Physician who sees in us what we cannot see, knows exactly where to place the knife. He cuts away that which we are most reluctant to give up. And how it hurts! But we must remember that pain is only felt where there is life, and where there is life is just the place where death is needed. Our Father wastes no time by cutting into parts which are already dead. Do not misunderstand me; He wants you to live abundantly, but this can only be accomplished by allowing Him to cut into that fleshly part of you which is still stubbornly clinging to life. (pp. 6–7)

Death to self must occur. The fourth step quickly follows: *resurrection* to something new. The Holy Spirit never removes something wrong from our lives without replacing it with something right. When Jesus takes over that number one position, He restores order. Where there was once spiritual death, spiritual life emerges. Pain and despair are given over to healing and hope. There is no end to the blessings Jesus brings into a life that allows Him to be Lord.

The death of self is not a work any one of us can accomplish on our own. It isn't even something which we desire in and of ourselves. It is the Holy Spirit who places such desires in our hearts. Praise God for that! I am so weak; He is so strong.

NO PERFECT MOMS

We need to be reminded that there are no perfect mothers or children. We have all fallen short of the glory of God. It is by God's grace that our children have made it. God's abundant grace and forgiveness brought us through the difficult times. So many times we are afraid of moving ahead because of what has happened in the past. We need to be reminded of the forgiving loving God who gives back to us "the years that the locust hath eaten" (Joel 2:25, KJV). All He wants from us is a repentant heart that says, "Yes, Lord. I have not always put You first in my life. My selfish desires have prevented me from being the mother You have desired. I'm sorry. I have lived my life for myself and not for You. Now make something beautiful out of the ashes of my life. I submit to Your control and lordship." Jesus will grant you back the "years that the locust hath eaten."

Virginia Satir in her book *Peoplemaking* (Science and Behavior Books, Inc.) describes the difficult task of being a mother.

> Parents teach in the toughest school in the world—the School for Making People. . . . There are few schools to train you for your job, and there is no general agreement on the curriculum. You have to make it up yourself. Your school has no holidays, no vacations, no unions, no automatic promotions or pay raises. You are on duty or at least on call 24 hours a day, 365 days a year, for at least 18 years for each child you have. . . . I regard this as the hardest, most complicated, anxiety ridden, sweat and blood producing job in the world. It requires the ultimate in patience, common sense, commitment, humor, tact,

love, wisdom, awareness and knowledge. At the same
time, it holds the possibility for the most rewarding,
joyous experience of a lifetime. (p. 197)

What a description! With no previous training, we try to
accomplish an almost impossible task, raising children. And
what makes it even more complicated is that often we are
striving to do it on our own without consulting the Lord. No
wonder we make so many mistakes!

OUR NEW GUINEA TRAINING CAMP
How often Warren and I reflect back on our life lived among the
Ipili tribe in the Western Highlands of New Guinea. In those
years I was given the freedom to be the mother my heart taught
me to be.

Living with four small children far from any type of medical
center often caused us great anxiety. Standing at my kitchen
window watching the airstrip slowly being engulfed in clouds in
the late afternoon would send shivers up my spine. With the
airstrip concealed from my view I knew a plane would never be
able to land. *What if one of my children or Warren became
seriously ill and needed emergency medical treatment? With
the airstrip inaccessible, it would be impossible to get them to
any hospital.* These thoughts continually went through my
mind. The memories of the struggles we experienced, periods
of loneliness, frustration, depression, and times of illness that
drove us to our knees in prayer are still vivid in my mind.

Arriving in New Guinea in 1967, Warren and I were like two
little children out to change the world, never suspecting God
would desire to change us. Little did we know that the Christian life was going to be so full of pressure-cooker experiences
and that New Guinea would be used by the Lord to mold us into
what He wanted us to become.

Holding me back from total surrender was fear and lack of

trust in a God who had plans only for my good and not evil (Jer. 29:11). Such a lack of surrender prevented me from entering into sweet communion with Jesus Christ and from experiencing His lordship in my life. My only alternative to hopelessness was to seek Jesus. Certainly He was more than willing . . . was I?

The mountains of New Guinea were to us very much like the oyster shell in which a pearl is formed. Encased in that shell, with all the irritations of life coming at us, we found God's love being layered upon us ever so gently. Through each difficult situation we were being taught that self had to be put aside. Jesus had to be first.

JEANNE'S CHALLENGE

For a period in my life I tried to keep God at a distance. As much as my love for God motivated me to serve Him, the cares of this world and the desires of my flesh were crowding Him out. I was a busy mother living in a primitive setting with four children under the age of six. I was a picture of nonstop motion; I convinced myself I had no time for an intimate relationship with Jesus.

God was not satisfied with that. He wanted me to see Him as my best friend, my Lord and Master. He wanted me to experience His love in my life and, most of all, His peace. To do that He sent people into my life to teach me.

Jeanne was just a mite of a woman. Standing only five feet tall and weighing less than 100 pounds, she appeared to be quite frail. Looks were deceiving though, for this tiny, unassuming woman became a powerful instrument of God's love to transform my life.

At first, I did not like her. She was a threat to my spirituality. Coming from an extremely conservative, traditional religious background, I shied away from people who were from different traditions. She expressed her faith in ways I was not accustomed to hearing. Her freedom in praising the Lord, her knowledge of the Scriptures, and her dedication to prayer often made me feel terribly insecure.

For some reason, Jeanne took a liking to me. Maybe it was her servant heart which wanted to reach out and help me as I struggled with four little ones. Being a mother herself of twin sons and two daughters, she understood my situation. Or maybe her sensitive spirit spotted the inner turmoil of my spiritual condition. She knew I was very religious but sensed my relationship with Jesus was not very personal. Something was holding me back from committing my life to Him. I look back and know the Holy Spirit revealed these things to her.

Despite my attempts to avoid being around her, she sought me out. At missionary gatherings and conferences she was right by my side, willing to help with the children and often providing housing for our entire family. I felt I was one of her special projects. The many long letters she wrote, constantly encouraging me to trust in the Lord, her mentioning of how much she remembered our family in her prayers, asking for God's blessings and protection upon us, and the countless numbers of Christian books she sent for me to read all confused me. Why was she being so diligent and kind? Why me? I certainly did not feel as if I needed all this encouragement. Being around her made me feel spiritually inadequate. I had never encountered anyone as expressive of her love for Jesus in both words and actions as this woman, and it scared me. I decided she was a fanatic and convinced myself this was not normal Christianity.

The more I was in the presence of Jeanne, the more I could not deny the fact there was something special about her. A quiet assurance, a genuine love for people, and a servant heart were what I was seeing. She was always there, reaching out in love, helping me understand how much God loved me.

She often tried to get me involved in spiritual activities such as Bible studies and retreats. Once she decided it would be a good idea if a retreat was planned for all the outstation wives of missionaries, which included me. How I resisted her invitation! No way was I going to put myself in such a vulnerable position. Those women would be able to see right through me. They all read their Bibles and prayed diligently; I didn't. They were all very spiritual; I wasn't. Up until now I had masked a lot of my spiritual inadequacies. I did not want to be found out. I used every excuse imaginable, but Jeanne wouldn't take no for an answer.

ANSWERED PRAYERS

The only way I figured I could get out of going and still save face was if the retreat were canceled. If it rained and rained hard, our airstrip would be inaccessible; I wouldn't be able to get a plane out of the Pogera. I, who prayed sporadically, began to pray with diligence, "Lord, please cause it to rain so that it will be impossible for me to go." I knew my prayer was selfish, but it was my last resort.

To my amazement, it began to rain. Roads were washed out, and Jeep travel became virtually impossible. It looked as though the retreat was off. Messages were being passed on our two-way radio. Unless the rain stopped by Wednesday, and the roads had a chance to be repaired, the women's retreat would have to be canceled. *Wow! This praying really does work*, I thought. Little did I realize that there was a group praying for just the opposite, and it was so ordered by God that they got their request.

Friday morning I found myself and our infant son John making the long, four-hour walk to our airstrip. I boarded a small Cessna plane to fly to my first retreat. Frightened and not knowing what to expect, I entered a room filled with 25 other women. I was so thankful to have Johnny in my arms. He was someone I could hold on to. He was my security.

When Jeanne saw me, she was filled with excitement. I'm sure I was the answer to one of her prayers. God had actually done it. I was there. Little did she know how hard I had prayed not to come. She sensed my fear and gave me a big hug. Almost immediately I began to feel God's love and peace in that room.

To this day I thank Him for not allowing my selfish prayer to be answered. Satan knew the effect this retreat would have on my relationship with Jesus Christ. He was out to prevent it from happening.

That night as we gathered for prayer (it was the first time I had ever experienced group prayer with people I did not know) I felt the presence of Jesus in the room. It was as though He and I were the only ones there. That weekend the Holy Spirit did a work in my life. The walls that surrounded me came tumbling down before the Lord. I was changed. I returned to my first love, Jesus.

There was a joy, a presence about me, that Warren noticed when I arrived home. I was filled with a quiet assurance of God's love and peace.

I have grown to love and appreciate Jeanne over the years. I refer to her now as my "spiritual Mom," the one who had the patience to stay with me and persevere in love despite my resistance. The Holy Spirit used her mightily.

In sharing this with you, I want you to understand how I too have struggled with my relationship with Jesus and how it has not always been easy, especially in the early years of mothering, to put Him first in my life. I know what it is like to soar to the heights with God, but I also know what it is like to be in the pits of despair. The Christian life is filled with challenges of all kinds. Just as soon as I feel I have everything in place, God seems to throw me a curve—an opportunity to learn and grow through His Spirit.

I know there are or will be people like Jeanne in your life. They will challenge you in your walk with the Lord. They may make you feel insecure. You may consider them to be fanatics, when in reality, there may be a deep need for you to draw closer to the Lord.

Without a personal relationship with Jesus Christ you can do nothing of any lasting value. You can't be the wife or mother you are supposed to be. Your time will not be spent profitably. You will be storing up treasures on earth that will only pass away (Matt. 6:19-21). Jesus wants to be first in your life. Your relationship with Him is to be your number one priority. If He doesn't hold that honored spot, attempts at other things will be futile—a waste of your time.

REFLECTING GOD'S GLORY

I believe with St. Augustine that "a Christian is to be an alleluia from head to foot." It is not something we can pretend to be. It is something that takes place in the quiet times we spend with the Lord. It happens as we come into His presence. The more time we spend alone with Jesus, the more we become like Him.

When Moses went up Mount Sinai to receive the Law of the Lord, he spent 40 days and 40 nights on the mountain in the presence of God. Exodus 33:18-23 records how Moses wanted very much to see the glory of the Lord. The Lord told Moses he would not be able to look upon the face of God, but He would hide Moses in the cleft of a rock and His glory would pass by. Moses was only permitted to see a glimpse of Him—just His back. When Moses came down from the mountain, his face shone so brightly that the Children of Israel could not look upon it (Ex. 34:29-30).

If we want to reflect the glory of the Lord to others, we need to spend time on the mountain with Him. "But we all, with unveiled face beholding as in a mirror the glory of the Lord, are being transformed into the same image from glory to glory, just as from the Lord, the Spirit" (2 Cor. 3:18).

It was the glory of Jesus I saw radiating from Jeanne's face.

Like Aaron and the Children of Israel, who were standing only at the foot of the mountain, I could not comprehend it. I had to be willing to climb the mountain and encounter God personally. No one else could do it for me. No matter how religious I was or how many years I had of Christian education, nothing would happen until I personally encountered God in the person of Jesus Christ. As long as I kept Him at a distance, I could not experience a relationship with Him.

Jesus was inviting me daily to come: "Behold, I stand at the door and knock; if any one hears My voice and opens the door, I will come in to him and will dine with him, and he with Me" (Rev. 3:20).

He longs for us to spend time with Him in sweet, uninterrupted communion. He is *always* there waiting. We are the ones who are too busy.

When Jesus becomes number one in your life, He will create within you the desire to set aside times to meet with Him, to get to know Him on a more intimate level. You will be challenged to practice His presence in your life on a daily basis.

Do you want a quality life? Do you want to be the best mother you can be? It can only come about as you personally encounter God. He must be your most important priority. By recognizing your sinfulness, accepting His forgiveness, and confessing Him as the Son of God, your Saviour and Lord, you move into a new level of living, called the "spirit-controlled" life. No longer desiring to be dominated by the desires of self or the world, you seek to live and react as Jesus would.

The walk up the mountain may be difficult, but if we persevere, every aspect of our lives will be positively affected. Spending time on the mountain with Him equips us to shine throughout the day in whatever we are called to do.

Chapter 8

A Time Set Apart

During the last months of our missionary term in New Guinea we lived on a station called Pausa with several other families. Since it was located near our mission's hospital, many missionaries would stay with us while they got medical attention.

Karen lived across a mud hole from us. She was the wife of a missionary teacher and mother of two very active toddlers. Always the one to volunteer first, her home became a haven for missionary families in need of lodging. She loved to entertain and enjoyed opening her home to strangers.

I certainly did not always have the same joy as Karen did for entertaining. It always required a lot of extra work. Bedding needed to be changed and washed, which wasn't an easy task, since it meant rising early to heat water, washing with a wringer washing machine, and then hanging it out to dry in a frantic race to beat the rain that came each afternoon. Extra guests meant extra cooking with long hours spent in front of a hot wood-burning stove baking bread and other needed items.

What did Karen have that I didn't? How did she get things

accomplished with such a happy attitude, and why did people enjoy staying in her home?

I discovered the answer to those questions once when I was preparing for a conference to be held on our station for outstation missionaries. Each family was responsible for housing a visiting family. I was frantically racing around trying to get things done, grumbling and complaining as usual. In the midst of making a cake, I discovered I was out of baking soda. With no store available, the next best place to get it would be from Karen. She was always prepared. With Johnny on my shoulders, I carefully made my way across the mud hole to Karen's, but she was gone. She had guests coming in just a few hours as I did—how could she afford to be away from her house? Her houseboy informed me that "the missus" had taken her Bible and gone for a walk. I thought she had to be crazy.

I was determined to find her. Off I went down the narrow road behind her house. There I found her sitting on a rock praying and reading her Bible. "What are you doing?" was my first question. "How can you afford to do this? Don't you know your guests will soon be arriving?"

She just looked at me and laughed. "By spending time alone with the Lord, I *am* preparing myself to be the kind of hostess He would want me to be. I want my home to be filled up with His love. Besides, everything gets done, and I'm not in a state of confusion doing it."

It was true. Karen did get things done. Her home always looked lovely, and she was known as one of the best cooks in the mission. Karen had found the secret of the balance between work and quiet time with the Lord. The busier she was, the more time she needed to be with Jesus.

I think of Karen as a modern-day Mary, who in the midst of busyness sought "the one thing needful" (Luke 10:38-42). She was willing to stop what she was doing to listen to the voice of Jesus. I was the Martha that day, and Jesus was saying: "Elise,

Elise, you are worried and bothered about so many things; but only a few things are necessary, really only one, for Karen has chosen the good part, which shall not be taken away from her."

TOO BUSY TO STOP

The Martha is so strong in most of us. When we are pressured by time, we feel that any quiet time would be a waste of time. There is always so much to do. Letting dishes remain in the sink for just 15 minutes longer while we escape to be alone with Jesus makes us feel guilty. We worry about what others will think, especially our neighbors, relatives, or friends. What if they make a surprise visit and find things out of order in our homes? Will they think we are lazy and unorganized? As a result, we start our day with busyness, putting off time with the Lord until later. Those quiet times keep being put off until later, but later never comes. Instead we find ourselves falling into bed exhausted and promising God that tomorrow will be different.

I have to admit, the Martha side of me appears more often than I would like. But there is a lot of Mary in me too. That desire to be alone with Jesus is a result of the Holy Spirit. He nudges and prompts me daily to stop what I am doing, to be obedient to His voice, and to open myself up to the blessings communion with Him brings.

After my first retreat experience in New Guinea I felt the need to get to know Jesus better. I did not know how to begin or what to do, but the desire was there, and whenever we desire spiritual things, the Holy Spirit will provide a way for them to become a reality in our lives. All we need to do is obey His promptings.

One day Jeanne challenged me. In her straightforward way, she said, "Elise, do you take out time to study God's Word? You need to allow God to equip you to be all He desires."

My first response to her was very cynical. "How can I find

time to read the Bible with four little ones constantly around me? You just don't understand."

She understood better than I thought, but in her gentle way she simply replied: "Well, if you don't feel you have the time, then ask God to help you find it."

It sounded like such a simple solution to a complex problem. Did Jeanne really understand how tired I was? Did she know how much I looked forward to afternoons and nap time with the children? Her children were older. Had she forgotten how difficult it was to wash floors with eight little hands trying to help? When the children were asleep, it was *my* time to rest or work without interruptions. Didn't she know I cherished that time alone?

I knew in my heart that Jeanne was right. A Christian was supposed to read her Bible and pray. My beautiful leather-bound, gilt-edged confirmation Bible, which at one time had been the treasure in my life, now lay dormant, a dust collector in my husband's study. The choice was mine. Either I could make a beginning and start reading or allow it to remain just another book on the shelf.

ABIDE IN HIM

I put God to the test that day. I challenged Him to do something I thought would be impossible. "OK, Lord. If You want me to start reading Your Word, You better find time for me to do it."

Shortly after I prayed, something strange happened. One o'clock in the afternoon was usually naptime. For two hours I would have uninterrupted peace and quiet. I cherished that time; I would actually be able to do something other than referee squabbles, wipe runny noses, change diapers, or feed children. One particular afternoon, I quickly began to scrub my kitchen floor at naptime. Suddenly, an urgency came upon me to stop what I was doing. I pushed it aside and kept scrubbing.

The next day the same thing happened. Finally, after the third time, I gave in to the Holy Spirit's prompting. I grabbed my Bible from the shelf, dusted it off, and began reading. My eyes fell upon John 15:4-5.

> Abide in Me, and I in you. As the branch cannot bear fruit of itself, unless it abides in the vine, so neither can you, unless you abide in Me. I am the vine, you are the branches; he who abides in Me, and I in him, he bears much fruit; for apart from Me you can do nothing.

The words jumped off the page. Was this what Jeanne had been trying to teach me? Why had I been so rebellious? With a repentant heart I came before the Lord confessing my disobedience and thanking Him for opening my eyes to see that without Him I could do nothing.

It was a quiet beginning, but I was on the right track. It has since been the source of strength in my mothering. It has been the answer to my problem of never seeming to have enough time. It is the only way I can exist in my world and still remain sane. Establishing a quiet time with the Lord actually saves time. How ironic it sounds! But it works. If you want a quality life, it can only come about as you spend quality time with the Lord.

SEEKING SILENCE

In today's society it is difficult to find truly quiet time. Even though we may not be listening to the radio, TV, or stereo, we may have them on. Background noise covers up our thoughts. Quiet forces us to deal with our thoughts.

Those of you who have teenage children know how they react to disappointments in their lives. They sit for hours listening to the radio or stereo in order to drown out their inner feelings. Women will go to crowded shopping centers to escape the quiet of their homes. We are afraid of being alone.

Everyone needs quiet, spiritual and physical quiet. Medical research has shown that meditation of some type slows the heart rate and lowers blood pressure. It can lower stress levels, which in turn decreases the risk of hypertension and heart attacks.

We often use the excuse that we really don't have the time to spend with Jesus. Our schedules are filled to capacity. Working mothers especially have every minute taken. This is where we need to be honest with ourselves and willing to ask God to show us His appointed time. It may come at a time when you usually watch TV, read the newspaper or your favorite magazine, or work around the house. The Holy Spirit may even prompt you to rise 15 minutes earlier each day to meet with God. If you are at all serious, God will help you find the time. When His prompting comes, you will have a choice. You can either obey and stop what you are doing, or disobey.

Mothers can be very creative in finding time to be with the Lord. Many times while nursing a baby, I would read my Bible. Quite often, on a rainy afternoon, instead of insisting my four little ones take their naps alone, I would give in and snuggle under the covers with them. As the rain beat upon our metal roof, I would read them a story about Jesus. They soon were gently lulled to sleep. Sometimes as they played a game on the kitchen floor, I would join them. As they became involved I would sit quietly and read or pray. When they were a little older, I bought each one a little pocket Bible. It was for them to read during our "Jesus time." While I read my Bible they pretended to read theirs. It made them feel so important!

As they got old enough to understand, they were told that Mommy was going to spend some time talking with Jesus in her quiet spot. They were to find something to do that would not disturb me during this time. I would set a timer for just five minutes. When it rang, they could interrupt me. Often while I prayed I heard them outside my door with the timer in their hands, anxiously waiting for it to ring.

Children can be taught to be patient for a short time. Use common sense in the amount of time you spend; five minutes to a three-year-old is an eternity. You may find it necessary to take several five minute breaks during the day—for praying, reading, praising, and just sitting quietly and listening to the Lord.

How blessed are the children who see their mother praying and studying God's Word. Mothers set examples for them to follow later in their own lives.

ESTABLISH A TIME

It is important to try to set aside the same time each day to meet with God. Once the habit is established it becomes a way of life. I find the morning hours best for me. Although rising early is difficult, I know that if I put off my quiet time until later, I will never get to it.

When my children were in grade school and high school, I made it a practice to rise just 15 minutes earlier each morning. It was such a temptation to shut the alarm off and have them come in and wake me up instead of me getting up before them. Stumbling into my dark kitchen was not very pleasant, but I was determined to spend time alone with the Lord. My goal was to prepare my home for the day. As I sat at my kitchen table, hair still uncombed and eyes half open, I entered into the holy of holies. There I brought each one of my children and Warren before the Lord in prayer. "Jesus," I would pray, "fill my home with Your love and presence today so that anyone entering will know You live here. As my husband and children enter this kitchen, let them feel Your presence. Help me to radiate Your love."

That time spent in the early morning transformed our household. Our four sleepy, sometimes irritable children were greeted by a mother who had just been in the presence of God. I was equipped by the Holy Spirit to be pleasant and loving, able to handle all the irritations that go along with getting children ready for school in the morning. I took the time to prepare a nutritious breakfast for them, and we had a time for family devotions. A time that was once chaotic was gradually transformed.

ESTABLISH A PLACE

It is important also to establish the same place for meeting with the Lord. It may be your kitchen table, the bathroom, your bedroom, the basement, a favorite chair in the living room, or some quiet spot outside. The Lord Jesus is not particular about the time and place. He is very flexible and will meet you anywhere at anytime. I meet often with the Lord at my kitchen table. I have a spot big enough for my notebook and Bible. If I start clearing dishes I am then tempted to wash them and get on with my day, so I leave them. Jesus doesn't mind dirty dishes, bread crumbs, or cereal boxes. All He is interested in is *you*.

You may not be able to spend a great amount of time in the beginning. If you are just starting, I suggest you spend 5 minutes sitting quietly before the Lord. You will soon find that it is not enough. Gradually, you will increase it to 15 or 30 minutes.

If you find it difficult to spend that much time, learn to segment your quiet time. You may find the early morning to be the best time for prayer. After the children leave for school, you may want to spend 15 minutes reading the Word. Later in the afternoon while the children are napping, you could spend time writing in your spiritual notebook. The evening, when the children are in bed, could be your time for praising Jesus.

This takes discipline. Conflict arises when we forfeit what we want to do for what God desires. We are convinced that in order to get something accomplished, we must be in constant motion. Stillness and quiet are contrary to our way of thinking.

DON'T GIVE UP!

In the beginning you will be restless and bored at times. Satan knows how effective and important quiet time is for your spiritual well-being. He will work to discourage you. Distractions of every kind will come your way: the telephone will ring, babies will cry, the children won't take their naps on schedule, and neighbors will stop over unexpectedly. Be disciplined and don't give up. Remember, Jesus understands. He was often hindered. The disciples were always looking for Him. Keep this principle in mind when you are ready to give up because of interruptions: an interrupted quiet time with Jesus is better than no quiet time.

Judy Eadie, a writer and cartoonist from Vancouver, British Columbia, wrote this beautiful description of what a mother's devotional life is sometimes like. It is called "Patchwork."

Lord, a quiet hour with You is like unrolling a bolt of exquisite new cloth.

On a frayed and matted morning like today I am craving again the smooth feel of an uninterrupted piece of praying. A length of solitude ample enough to really spread my life out on, and cut into with gusto.

In the past I've stocked my share of expensive serenities. Sometimes at night I have been with You, laying out flawless, saved up hours as if they were a roll of purple satin. The family is in bed, the clock ticking, I am free to display before You all my hoarded meditations, to pin each difficulty in place on the vivid stretch of silence. Spaciousness, Lord, for creative communion.

But lately there have been these shapeless scraps of quiet, endless irritating bits and pauses hardly big enough to pin a hallelujah to. My mind has become a scrap bag of remnant prayers, torn off.

Intercessions, snippets of Scripture. And You know me, the sulky perfectionist, wasting the million small moments while pining for the grand opportunity.

So instead of luxuriating in yard upon shimmering yard of uninterrupted meditation, I find myself with a thrift-shop jumble of small amounts to praise You with.

Teach me, Jesus, what to do with them. Piece them together like stained glass, and make something beautiful of all the little patchwork pleas and praises of my day.*

Can you identify with Judy? I have been through those times at two separate stages in my life—as a young mother of four children and as an older mother of four older children and a baby. It does not get any easier as you get older. But this too will pass.

An 86-year-old, saintly woman approached me several years ago after a conference I had done on time. On a crumpled piece of paper, she had written, "Make sure of your relationship with God while you are young and full of busyness because the time will come when all the busyness will be over and God is your only companion—you will not be lonely." She knew how quickly time passes and how important it is to establish a relationship with God early in life.

A SPIRITUAL NOTEBOOK

I strongly suggest you develop a spiritual notebook. In Psalm 102:18 the psalmist tells why he is recording Israel's history. "This will be written for the generation to come; that a people yet to be created may praise the Lord." That's kind of the way I

---

*This article is taken from *Decision* magazine March 1976, © 1976 Billy Graham Evangelistic Association. Used by permission. All rights reserved.

feel about my spiritual notebook. I want it to be a legacy for my children. In reading it they will be encouraged to see how God has worked in the life of one ordinary woman, their mother.

Martin Luther stressed many years ago the importance of keeping a spiritual notebook or journal. Walter Trobisch writes of this in his little booklet, *Martin Luther's Quiet Time* (InterVarsity Press).

> Indeed, those who get used to the discipline of having their quiet time with a notebook are not likely ever to give it up. What makes our devotional life so unattractive and boring is the fact that each day, every one of us has just about the same kind of general, vague pious thoughts. This causes monotony. Our thoughts remain distant and abstract and do not come to grips with our concrete daily life. The writing down, as Luther suggests, is a form of the incarnation of God's Word. It becomes tangible, visible and concrete. It forces us to be precise, definite and particular. Monotony is replaced by variety and surprise. Taking notes enables us also to check whether we have carried out what we planned in the morning. (p. 19)

Keep your notebook with your Bible. Divide it into sections, such as Bible study, prayer requests, letters to God, thoughts from God, lessons I'm learning, praises and thank yous, and family memories.

Begin your quiet time by sitting silently before Him. Try to clear your mind of other thoughts. Breathe deeply and relax. Martin Luther refers to this time as a period of warming up. He believed that God speaks to us through our thoughts when the "heart is warmed up." Concentrate on God's goodness and love. Look to the cross and meditate on the love Christ showed for you in His death. Think about His greatness. Dwell on His attributes. Write them down.

Come before the Lord with a repentant heart. Confess your sins before Him. (Psalm 66:18 says: "If I regard wickedness in my heart, the Lord will not hear.") Don't pass over this step quickly. Allow the Holy Spirit to do His work. Ask Him to show you any attitudes you need to change. Confess your sins and accept the forgiveness Jesus has won for you. Write down anything God shows you in this area in your notebook.

Next, begin to read God's Word. List on your notebook page the date and the passage you read. Write out your thoughts on what you have read. Don't be discouraged if nothing comes. I have several pages in my notebook with nothing on them, except the date and record of what I read. For days at a time nothing new may come. This does not mean God is not working. Be persistent during these "dry times."

Ask for the Holy Spirit to guide you as you read the Word and to reveal Jesus to you. Remember, the Bible is a divinely inspired book and cannot be fully understood apart from the Spirit's teaching. We need Him to illumine our thoughts.

If you read three chapters every day for about one year, you can read through the entire Bible. Is that one of your goals? You can do it in about 15 minutes a day. I try to read one chapter in the New Testament and one in the Old Testament each day. I also keep the Psalms and Proverbs in my reading schedule throughout the year.

Try writing your feelings to God in the form of a letter. I used to be self-conscious about doing this, but God is not concerned with punctuation, capitalization, or sentence structure. Write your thoughts, what you are feeling, and the struggles you are experiencing. For the present, no one else is going to read this, so be honest with God. (I do shy away from using names of other people. I use only initials, just in case someone reads it accidentally.)

Writing is excellent therapy. Once you get it down on paper it is off your mind. On those nights when I am not able to go to sleep, I get out of bed and write out my thoughts on paper. That usually helps me get back to sleep.

I reread my letters to God periodically. What a joy to know God has worked so miraculously in my life and taught me so much! Many little details that I would have otherwise easily forgotten 'are recorded there for me to remember.

I have a section in my notebook just for memories. Memory is such a beautiful gift from the Lord. In this section, I have recorded each one of my children's birthdays and how they were celebrated, their first days of school each year, their first dates, our vacation times, and other special events. They are written in the form of thank-you letters to God. We often promise to keep record of the many cute things our children say and do; this is an excellent place for that.

I devote another section in my notebook to prayer requests. When someone asks me to pray, I write it down immediately with the date next to it. Often in my silent time with God, He places someone before me for the purpose of praying for them. Beside each request I write down the date of God's answer with a big PTL ("praise the Lord") next to it.

Offer the Lord what you have to give. He will never turn you away. He will teach you to develop the time you do have and turn it into something beautiful, which will bless your family and those around you. Your life will exhibit order. You will be able to tell the difference between the urgent and important. Because of your quiet time you will be prepared to operate your home with God's direction. It will take a step of faith to begin, but trust God that His blessings will follow.

Chapter 9

Time in the Midst of Ministry

It is not God who loads us until we bend or crack with an ulcer, nervous breakdown, heart attack, or stroke. These come from our inner compulsions coupled with the pressure of circumstances. . . . If the Christian is too busy to stop, take spiritual inventory, and receive his assignments from God, he becomes a slave to the tyranny of the urgent. He may work day and night to achieve much that seems significant to himself and others, but he will not finish the work *God* has for him to do. (Charles E. Hummel, "The Tyranny of the Urgent," InterVarsity Press, pp. 11-12)

T he rapid ascent of the 727 airliner made the scenery outside take on the appearance of a massive blur. I tried to focus but soon had to turn my head. Once airborne, a feeling of peacefulness surrounded me. Now as I gazed out the window to the scenery below, the terrain appeared almost motionless, lying in stillness and tranquility.

A strange picture of my life, I thought. My fast-paced living was causing everything around me to blur. Once again I was finding myself in turmoil; the pressures of life were assaulting me. I wondered why I was even on a plane, going to Omaha for a women's retreat: how could I give any more of myself to anyone? Physical, mental, and, worst of all, spiritual exhaustion had taken over. It seemed everyone wanted a part of me, and there was just nothing left to give. I was depressed, unhappy, and experiencing all of the typical signs of burnout. My family needed me. My church needed me. Everywhere I looked, people desperately needed help.

"TAKE TIME TO SEEK ME"

The ministry God had called me to should not have been this burdensome. Serving the Lord was to bring joy, not grumbling and complaining. In my desperation I once again cried out to the Lord. "Lord, what am I to do? I'm so weary. All I want to do is run away from it all."

In the quietness of my heart the Lord spoke. "Elise, why is it you always want to run away only when the pressure gets so great you cannot stand it anymore? You are running away from Me too. Instead, run first to Me; then you will be able to cope with the pressure. Take time to seek Me."

The Holy Spirit slowly opened my eyes to see what had been taking place in my life. I had become so busy serving the Lord that I didn't take time anymore to be with Him. No wonder I felt drained! I was depending on my own strength, not His. The ministry He had called me to had come between us.

The Lord might have said to me what He said to the church in Ephesus in Revelation 2:2-4.

I know your deeds and your toil and perseverance, and

that you cannot endure evil men . . . and you have perseverance and have endured for My name's sake, and have not grown weary. But I have this against you, that you have left your first love.

I who loved Jesus so much and felt so free to serve Him now looked upon Him as my taskmaster. Where had those sweet moments of fellowship gone? I knew Jesus had freed me from the trap of trying to earn His favor, yet I was groaning under the weight of good works, hoping He would love me more. I had once felt accepted based on His love alone; I was now trying to prove to God and others how spiritual I was.

He was not the one driving me to the point of exhaustion. My own aspirations and desires were at the root of my problem. All He required from me was to be in love with Him.

Barry Gruters, in an article entitled, "When 'Ministry' Comes between You and God" (*Discipleship Journal*, Issue 13, 1983), says this:

I have observed that as believers become increasingly skilled and involved in ministry activities, many actually spend *less* time alone with the Lord. Ministry activities can in fact become a justification for a growing distance in our relationship with God.

As a result, our personal ministry becomes only a product of the flesh, and not the product of abiding in and depending on Christ. It is a shallow ministry, and a short-term ministry.

The solution is to take the time, even if it must be taken away from ministry activities, to restore our full commitment to intimacy with Christ—not only for the sake of personal growth, but also for the sake of our ministries.

I knew the solution to my problem was to take time from my

busy schedule to restore fellowship, commitment, and intimacy with Christ, even if it meant having to say no to those who needed me. I needed to be filled up with Jesus.

Isn't that exactly what Jesus did in His ministry? When the crowds pressed in around Him, He withdrew to the wilderness or to the sea to seek fellowship with His Heavenly Father. Jesus did not heal everyone in Palestine, but He did do what His Father wanted Him to do.

TIME TO RETREAT

Seated next to me on the plane was a young woman. The dove pin on her suit lapel gave me an indication she might be Christian. The aisle seat was occupied by a casually dressed, middle-aged man. Once we were in the air, he appeared to be asleep.

I was not yet prepared to enter into conversation with the woman next to me. In my hand was the book *Celebration of Discipline* by Richard J. Foster (Harper and Row), and I was determined to get some reading done.

I am amazed at God's timing. He seems to always be full of surprises. The words I was reading seemed to jump right off the pages. Was this something I should be underlining and circling and imprinting on my mind?

Some of my most profitable experiences of study have come through structuring a private retreat for myself. Usually it involves two to three days. No doubt you will object that given your schedule you could not possibly find that kind of time. I want you to know that it is no easier for me to secure that time than for anyone else. I fight and struggle for every retreat, scheduling it into my datebook many weeks in advance. I have suggested this idea to groups and found that professional people with busy schedules, laborers with rigid schedules, housewives with large families, and others can, in fact, find time for a private study retreat. I have discovered that the most difficult problem is not finding time but convincing myself that this is important enough to find the time. . . .

The best place is anywhere as long as it is away from home. To leave the house not only sets you free from the telephone and domestic responsibilities but it also sets your mind into a learning mode. . . . Often Catholic retreat centers are receptive and can accommodate private retreatants. (pp. 60–61)

I was interrupted by the flight attendant asking me if I desired something to drink. Laying aside my book, I turned to the young woman next to me and we began to chat. After talking about various things, she asked me why I was going to Omaha. "For a women's retreat," I replied.

"Oh, I used to go on retreats as a child," she said, "but I never really appreciated them until I got older."

She was from an Episcopal background. I could tell that our ideas of a retreat were two different things. What I was going to lead was really a conference for women who were gathered for a weekend of fellowship, the study of God's Word, and relaxation. We called them retreats, but in reality they were conferences for the purpose of learning.

We then began to talk about our personal views on the concept of retreating. I shared with her the time Claudette, my Christian neighbor, invited me to retreat with her to one of the nearby Catholic retreat centers. I made up every excuse imaginable. I knew what she meant by retreating—being still and quiet for an entire day. I, who was used to constant motion, would never survive. Private retreats just were not my thing.

While we were talking, the gentleman next to her opened his eyes for a moment, but then appeared to fall back to sleep, uninterested in our conversation. "Have you ever gone on a personal retreat?" the woman asked me.

I replied that I hadn't, but had lately been feeling the need to escape. I described the frustration I was experiencing in regard to time pressure.

At that moment, the gentleman sitting next to her decided to join in the discussion. "You'll have to excuse me for interrupting your conversation, but I have been listening to both of you discuss this concept of retreating and I feel I have something to offer. I am a Jesuit priest from the University of Detroit and my position there is Retreat Director. I direct many Christians in personal spiritual retreats, some of them lasting as long as five days."

You can imagine how surprised we were. I believe God had arranged this special meeting of Christians on this plane. Once again, He manifested His love for me in providing a learning experience and someone to teach me.

We spent the remainder of that flight discussing the benefits of retreating. The priest challenged me to take out time from my busy schedule to retreat. He said that the busier I get with ministry, the more I need time alone with the Lord to seek His direction. He challenged me to plan a personal retreat soon.

I used every excuse possible. First, I explained that I was a very busy wife and mother. "It just wouldn't work in my family," I said. "Warren just wouldn't go for watching our four children while I take off. It's just not feasible."

I gave some other excuses, but none of them was good enough for this man of God. Finally he turned to me and said with a holy boldness, "It's not that you don't have the time or that your commitment to your family is so great. The real reason is that you don't feel it is valuable enough, and second, you have a fear of being alone with God." I was shocked. A total stranger was able to see right through me. Was God using this man to speak to me about what was missing in my life?

The puzzle pieces were beginning to fit together. In a two-hour period I had been taught a fundamental principle for anyone who serves the Lord: *The busier I become serving the Lord, the more time I need to spend with Jesus*. Wasn't it Martin Luther who said that he usually spent two hours a day studying the Word, except on exceptionally busy days, when he spent four.

Jesus instructs us to "seek first His kingdom and His righteousness; and all these things shall be added to you" (Matt. 6:33). Take time to be holy in the midst of your daily duties. Take out time to seek the Lord.

In the midst of an active life comes the call to draw away quietly and encounter God in all His glory and majesty. How irrational this is to our way of thinking! *I've got to get things done,* we think. *I have to constantly be doing something in order to be productive and successful.*

HE LONGS FOR US

Can you imagine Jesus longing to have you all to Himself? Can you envision Him sitting at your kitchen table or in your living room patiently waiting to spend time with you? Can you see the smile on His face, even when you're rushing around trying to get everything done and neglecting Him? Can you see His arms unfold and beckon you to come? He wants you near. He wants to tell you how much He loves you. Why do we deny ourselves the joy of His fellowship and get so caught up in what self desires? Each time we turn away from His beckoning, we deprive ourselves of the blessings He intends to give. We actually waste time as we run around in circles accomplishing nothing.

"Communion with Jesus is high on our list of spoken values, but seldom on our list of things to do." Tim Fallon, in an article entitled "Too Busy to Pray" (*Religious Teacher's Journal*, March 1983), gives insight into why it is so difficult to set aside time with the Lord.

Busyness, distractions, lack of ability, and doubts about the effectiveness of prayer are some of the many symptoms of why we don't pray. The root cause goes far deeper, affecting us at the core of our persons. We don't pray because to pray is to enter into conflict. . . . Because of the pain of facing these conflicts, we grab any excuse that will protect us from the invasion of God. (p. 42)

He goes on to say that in our society, power and control are valued. The self-starter, the initiator, the person who gets things done, is affirmed. By contrast, spending time alone with the Lord is an act of surrender. It forces us to forfeit our own agendas and resist the urge to take charge.

Fallon goes on to say that we are also told in our society that productivity is what counts. Being alone with God in quiet contradicts this by emphasizing quiet over activity.

We are also duped to believe that since our culture is rooted in anxiety, stress is part of the normal lifestyle. Fallon believes that

our addiction to adrenaline has reached epidemic proportions. Prayer is difficult because it calls us to radical trust in the face of any adversity. . . . We may curse our stress-filled lives, but we would rather cling to them than to risk the trust required to give them up. (p. 41)

HEART CONTACT WITH THE LORD

Many mothers I talk to feel they can talk to the Lord while they work. After all, the command is to "pray without ceasing" (1 Thes. 5:17). True, we are to be in prayer at all times, but we also need quiet time away from anything that would distract us from listening to the Lord.

I often use the example of my relationship with Warren to show how we get so busy that we don't really listen to the Lord.

There are times when he comes home, and I am a bundle of energy. He wants to talk, and I want to keep on working. He follows me around the house as I work and tries to communicate. No eye contact is established, and there is very little response from me because I am so preoccupied with what I am doing. I'm sure many of you experience this when you want to tell your husband something and he either has his eyes on the television set or his head buried in the newspaper.

Being quiet before the Lord is not so much an opportunity for us to talk to Him and bring our needs before Him as it is a chance to listen to Him speak. We can talk to the Lord anywhere, anyplace, and anytime, while we work or play. He always gives us His undivided attention. He hears us no matter how busy we are. What He wants is our undivided attention. He wants us to be still enough to hear His voice speak those beautiful words of love in the depths of our being. He wants to establish "heart contact," just as my husband desires eye contact. It is in this quiet that we receive His direction for our lives and also understanding in His Word. It is in our quiet spot where we hear Him saying, "My child, I love you."

TITHING OUR TIME

In Malachi 3:8-10 we find a beautiful promise from the Lord regarding tithing. Growing up with the tithing principle in my life has allowed me to see God's miraculous provision for all my needs. Our family has adopted this principle and we have seen the blessings of God in abundance. It takes a step of faith to believe that God can act in such a way, though. Letting go of any of what we have causes pain. That's why tithing is so difficult. If this is true for material things, can it also be true for the time He has allotted to us?

"Will a man rob God? . . . Bring the whole tithe into the storehouse, so that there may be food in My house, and test Me now in this," says the Lord of hosts, "if I will not open for you the windows of heaven, and pour out for you a blessing until there is no more need."

Bring the whole tithe of your time before God and put Him to the test to see if He will not open the windows of heaven and give you enough time until there is no more need. God is faithful to His promises.

You as a mother are in constant ministry to others. You can't escape that fact. Your husband and children take up a great amount of your time. But there may also be many others who come to you for advice or who just want to talk over a cup of coffee. I think we would be amazed at the number of kitchen tables used daily as counseling centers for hurting children, family members, neighbors, and friends. I wonder how many cups of coffee have been drunk while someone tells another of the hurts in their hearts. I wonder how many hours have been spent on the phone trying to encourage someone to hang in there just a little while longer.

Women, I believe, have a unique quality about them that causes them to want to reach out and love the world. We have a sensitive spirit, a gentleness about us that draws people to share with us their hurts and joys. We would fix everyone's problems if it were possible. That quality of love coupled with God's love can make any woman a dynamic tool in the hands of God.

God wants to use us in the lives of others, to reach out with His love. But beware—unless we spend time drawing close to Him and drawing on His strength and wisdom in times of quiet, we will easily fall into the trap of having a self-oriented ministry. That is when burnout takes place.

RETREAT AT HOME

You may be one who would give anything just to spend three

days on a retreat somewhere, but your only hope for retreat is to go into your bathroom and close the door. Even that brings no solitude, because your little ones are sitting outside the door begging to come in.

Many young mothers do not have the privilege of going on a private retreat. They may not have the needed support of a husband, or the responsibilities facing them may be overwhelming. We still need to be reminded that we can encounter Jesus daily as we retreat in the privacy of our homes to seek His face and hear Him whisper His words of love.

Our private retreat centers can be our bathrooms, bedrooms, kitchens, or basements. The surroundings don't make a whole lot of difference to God. *You* are the one He is interested in. He will meet with you anywhere, anytime. Just do it! The refreshment you receive will equip you to do the work He has called you to do.

I have taken the challenge and scheduled in time for personal retreating. There is a lovely Jesuit retreat center not far from my home that has become a place for restoring my soul. But even more precious are those quiet moments I spend with the Lord on a daily basis. Because I want to listen to the voice of my Heavenly Father, I am learning to do His will.

SMOOTH FLYING AT HIGH SPEEDS

Back in 1980, my life was going 100 mph and nothing was going right. I was on the verge of burnout. Today my life is going six times faster, yet I am able to handle the pressures. With three children in college, a daughter soon to be married, a son in high school, and a precious four-year-old, I teach Bible studies, lead conferences, write, maintain our home, and keep the fires of love burning in our family. My life is busy, yet there is a peacefulness, tranquility, and joy about it. Despite the fast pace, I am able to handle life's pressures. Why? Because I have found the answer in soaring to the heights with God.

I asked a friend who is also a professional pilot how fast a jet is traveling at takeoff. "About 100 mph," was his reply. "Flying at an altitude of approximately 30,000 feet, the speed is about 600 mph—six times greater."

Isn't it ironic that with greater speed there can be peacefulness? I believe that is a beautiful picture of life led by the Holy Spirit. We can be busy and yet know order in our lives. The secret lies in soaring to the heights with God. When we are at ground level, the pace at which we are traveling will seem frantic. It is not the busyness of life that causes us to burn out; it is the inability to recognize our need to be alone with God. For in this aloneness we receive the Father's will for our lives. In this seclusion we realize we are nothing without Him. The answer to the pressure problem is retreating into the presence of God and in silence, listening to His voice. Never underestimate the importance of being alone with God. The busier you are, the more time you need to spend with Him.

I believe mothers need this just as much as any pastor, teacher, or evangelist. We are responsible for the lives of people. We hold the future of our world in our arms and on our laps. You are important to the Lord as you minister to the world by ministering in your home.

Do you want to get more out of your time? Invest it in your relationship with Jesus, and see how He will "open for you the windows of heaven, and pour for you a blessing until there is no more need" (Mal. 3:10).

We need to find God, and He cannot be found in noise and restlessness. God is the friend of silence. See how nature—trees, flowers, grass—grow in silence. See the stars, the moon and sun, how they move in silence. Is not our mission to give God to the poor in the slums? Not a dead God, but a living, loving God. The more we receive in silent prayer, the more we can give in our active life. We need silence to be able to touch souls. The essential thing is not what we say, but what God says to us and through us. All our words will be useless unless they come from within—words which do not give the light of Christ increase the darkness.

Mother Teresa

Chapter 10

Wife First, Mother Second

One of the most difficult places to act like a Christian is in the family. Human nature makes us think that our rights are more important than everyone else's. When our rights are violated, we fight to preserve them.

God's will for the family is for each person to "put on a heart of compassion, kindness, humility, gentleness and patience; bearing with one another, and forgiving each other" (Col. 3:12-13). When these attributes of Christ begin to be lived out by the members of a family, the home becomes a refuge for its members, a place where Jesus lives and loves, a training ground and one of the primary workshops of the Holy Spirit.

It is no secret that the family is under attack by Satan. His ways are devious and subtle, and he will stop at nothing to destroy what God has ordained as good. He knows that in the context of the Christian family servanthood, commitment, forgiveness, love, submission to authority, praying for one another, humility, and many of the attributes of Christ are instilled in the minds of its members, especially the children. By destroying the order of the Christian family, Satan hits at the very core of both spiritual and human survival.

We mothers must be prepared to protect our families from the onslaught of the world and Satan. As modern-day Nehemiahs we must be ready to stand firm, with the sword of the Spirit (the Word of God) in one hand and the tools given to us from the Holy Spirit to build the walls of our home in the other hand. We are to be in the process of reconstructing. I cannot stress too much how important this is for mothers to realize. The mother is the heartbeat of the home. She sets the tone. If she does not give her family a higher priority than her other activities and commitments, she is setting her home up for confusion and disorder, with the possibility of destruction in the future.

THE ORDERED FAMILY

God's order for the family starts with Christ. He is first in the line of order. "Christ is the head of every man, and the man is the head of a woman, and God is the head of Christ" (1 Cor. 11:3). Jesus is to be head of the household. He is the final authority. This is what makes a Christian home different from others. Parents seek direction from Jesus as they make decisions. His lordship is recognized and family members submit to His authority.

The Scriptures then go on to say that the husband is "the head of the wife" (Eph. 5:23). In today's society this principle is greatly spurned. It seems archaic. Rebellion rises to the surface when this issue is discussed, even among Christian women. "No one is going to rule over me," many respond. Yet it is this very principle, properly understood, accepted, and put into practice, that brings order to a home.

The headship of the husband is not to be domineering. It is not superiority (Gal. 3:28; Gen. 2:24). Instead, it is loving leadership that places the needs of others, especially the needs of his wife, before his own. Husbands are told to love their wives as Christ loved the church and gave up His life for it (Eph. 5:25).

WEAKER VESSELS

In 1 Peter 3:7 husbands are told to live with their wives in an understanding way. The wife is described as a "weaker vessel," and she is to be given honor as a "fellow-heir of the grace of life." Many women take this to be an insult; to them it implies inferiority.

The term "weaker vessel" is not, however, used in a derogatory way. We as women know we are capable of great emotional strength and fortitude. We are often strong when our husbands are weak. "Weaker vessel" is used to help men understand the high, honored place of importance a woman is to have in the home. In Jewish homes many types of vessels were used daily. Some were big sturdy pots. Placed at the entrance way of each home, they contained water for cooking and washing. These pots were accustomed to much use and abuse. Other vessels were more fragile. These were used as vases and containers for valuable pieces of jewelry. Because of their beauty and delicacy, they were given places of honor in the home and carefully protected.

Can you see the symbolism? As women, we are depicted as beautiful, delicate, fragile containers that hold cherished items. Our husbands are required by God to protect us from any abuse the world may bring and give us a place of honor in the home.

This headship has nothing to do with status, equality, or superiority. It has everything to do with *function*. I perform a different function in the life of my family than my husband. My function does not discredit my status; it does not mean I am subordinate or inferior.

A WILLING SERVICE

As wives we are called by God to live in loving submission to our husbands as unto the Lord (Eph. 5:22; Phil. 2:5-9; Col. 3:18; 1 Peter 3:1). This is not a master-slave relationship, but a relationship that requires a servant-heart. A slave has no choice or free will. A servant does; she chooses to place herself under authority.

This submissive role is conceived first in the heart. It is the "hidden person of the heart, with the imperishable quality of a gentle and quiet spirit, which is precious in the sight of God" (1 Peter 3:4).

Submission manifests itself in a willingness to serve. This humble attitude is described in Philippians 2:3.

Do nothing from selfishness or empty conceit, but with humility of mind let each of you regard one another as more important than himself; do not merely look out for your own personal interests, but also for the interests of others.

We convince ourselves that submissiveness manifests itself only in action. This repels us: "Do you mean I am always going to have to pick up his dirty underwear and socks? Will it mean I will have no say in family matters—how we raise our kids, spend our money, or where we take vacations? I don't want to become a doormat."

We become gripped with fear when we are asked to take a step of faith in this area. Our preconceived ideas and fears prevent us from receiving the blessings submission can bring. Remember, submissiveness is not so much an action as it is an attitude of the heart. Once the heart receives it, God gives us the wisdom to live it out.

Confusion, misspent energy, and wasted time are all by-products of a woman's refusal to live with God's order for the family. In her rebellion she allows herself as a "weaker vessel" to be in the position of those big, heavy, thick water pots in a

Jewish home. They get bumped and sometimes kicked. A fragile vase could never withstand that type of treatment. Eventually it gets broken.

My husband is a man of great leadership ability. He also comes from German descent, which may or may not explain his willingness to be the head of the house. Early in our marriage this was established, and early in our marriage I rebelled. We reminisce about the difficulties we encountered as a result. After many years of marriage, I have come to accept his loving leadership and the protection, respect, love, and freedom it has brought.

Even though he is the God-appointed head of our home, I have to remind him that every head must sit on a neck, and I am that neck that turns the head. I influence him greatly and have learned over the years how important I am in the decision-making process of our home.

THE ROLE OF CHILDREN

With the husband as head of the wife and the wife living in loving submission to her husband, the children then come under the authority of both mother and father. Again, this has nothing to do with status. It has everything to do with order and function.

Children were never intended to devastate a marriage. God's intent was for children to be a blessing. Yet, in many marriages, parents allow children to interfere with their love relationship. When children are placed above either spouse, priorities get out of order, resulting in frustration, confusion, and wasted time and energy.

Many husbands begin to play second fiddle when children arrive on the scene. Where once he had a wife who listened attentively to his idle conversation, she now shows little interest. At one time she took pride in her appearance. Now she greets him at the door with hair uncombed, wearing blue jeans and a sweatshirt with baby burp on it. The admiration he once received is now directed to the children and the cute things they say and do.

At the same time the wife is beginning to feel the weight of being a mother of small children. She becomes envious of her husband, who appears to have a great deal of free time to spend on himself while she is a captive in her own home. At one time her husband was attentive, admiring, and thoughtful. Now he seems remote. The newspaper, TV, and activities outside the home become his means of escape. She feels used, unappreciated, and unloved. These feelings usually manifest themselves in their sexual relationship. It may be the first thing on his mind, but the last on hers. Headaches, exhaustion, and the need for sleep become excuses. They feel resentful and bitter rather than warm and loving.

In the beginning years of our marriage, Warren and I encouraged each other and listened attentively as the other expressed his or her feelings. Our worlds revolved around each other. We dreamed about the future, counted our pennies together, and made plans to turn our world upside down for Christ.

Our first child, Paul, was born in our second year at seminary. The doctor said as he delivered him, "This one looks like a general." The doctor's prediction was right. From the time of his birth, Paul commanded attention.

My mom and dad came for a visit shortly after Paul was born. It totally amazed us how one baby required four adults to care for him. He cried day and night. After mom and dad left, he continued crying for three months with colic. Motherhood was not what I had anticipated. Paul was a demanding child who required much attention, discipline, and love.

During that time I received a letter from a dear aunt. It read,

The new daddy feels like the most neglected, unloved,

taken for granted, unimportant fellow in the world. And that he is when the new baby comes! He rates second, but with patience, understanding and helpfulness, it won't be long and he will be first again.

David was born 17 months later, Elisabeth arrived 22 months after David, and John 23 months after Elisabeth. I was exhausted. Warren was a good father and tried to help as much as possible, but it never seemed to be enough. Even though I loved and enjoyed my children and husband, nagging and complaining became my favorite pastime.

Tension began to mount in our home. My priorities became jumbled. At the top of my list were my children. I worked day and night to ensure their comfort and meet their needs. Next in line was me. I fought for my rights and rebelled against my husband's authority. At the bottom of the list came Warren. It almost seemed as if I was intentionally blocking him out. I looked at him as a mature adult quite capable of caring for himself—he didn't need me! The more I threw my life into my children, the more Warren spent time at his work. It was a vicious cycle.

Communication began to break down. Instead of sharing feelings, we shared information about what had transpired during the day. Warren was not interested in how many times Paul teased Elisabeth or that John finally learned to put his toys away. He wanted me to notice *him*. All I wanted was his love and encouragement, not information about the baby chickens he had just ordered for the mission agricultural project.

We were like two strangers. Too preoccupied with our own thoughts and needs, we didn't take time to listen or respond to each other. Those were difficult years in our marriage, as they are in most young couples' lives. I had become a mother first and a wife second, placing the needs of my children above those of my husband.

EMERGENCY!

It was an ordinary morning in New Guinea. The roosters began to crow at the break of dawn. Warren was awake but lay almost motionless beside me. His forehead was covered with beads of perspiration. I sensed something was wrong. "Warren, are you OK?" In a shallow, shaking voice he answered, "Elise, I'm really in a lot of pain and can't move. I don't know what's wrong. You had better call for a doctor on the two-way radio."

Panic gripped me. It was 6:00 A.M. I would have to wait until 7:30 A.M. before I could contact anyone. As we waited, the pain became increasingly worse. At times Warren began to drift in and out of consciousness. He desperately needed medical attention soon.

The children were beginning to wake up one by one. They sensed something was wrong and as a result, would not leave my side. In the midst of chaos, I tried to move calmly from one thing to the next. My pace, however, began to speed up. Many things needed to be done before we left the station. Once we left, I knew it would be weeks before we would be able to return. Things had to be left in order: I had to appoint someone to take care of the chickens and ducks, turn off and clean the kerosene refrigerator, pack suitcases, and wash dirty diapers. Even as I worked feverishly, I couldn't help but think about the possibility of Warren dying.

It seemed an eternity until I could call for help, but when I did, the sound of familiar voices on the other end gave me great comfort. "This is 'Sierra Charlie' calling. Can you read me? My husband is very ill and needs to get to a hospital. This is an emergency. I need help."

Immediately, I was put in contact with our mission doctor. Strangely enough I found myself having the ability to think clearly, as symptoms were relayed and information given on what was to follow. God's strength was there. With all four children crying, the Ipili people insisting that they see Warren

129

before he die so they could cry, and Warren groaning from the extreme pain, I was able to prepare our home and family for the inevitable helicopter evacuation.

The comforting voice of the doctor interrupted the confusion around me. "We have made arrangements for a helicopter to evacuate Warren to the Pogera airstrip. From there a small single engine plane will fly him to a hospital on the coast of New Guinea. There is only one problem. The plane is small and can only accommodate your husband, you, and your infant son. If you decide to go with your husband, your other children must remain in the Pogera. There is no room for them on the plane."

HUSBAND OR CHILDREN?

Of course I would go with Warren. But leave my children? That was impossible—there was no one I could leave them with. Was this doctor oblivious to our situation? Did he not know about outstation living and the bush? I felt torn apart.

God knew my turmoil and provided a possible solution to my dilemma. Karen and Paul Vollrath lived about three and a half hours from our home on foot, on the top of the next mountain. Their home was just one and a half hours from the airstrip. If I could get my children to the airstrip, they could pick them up there.

I called them on the two-way radio. Yes, they would do that. The only catch was that our children would have to be left in the care of the New Guineans at the airstrip for an hour or so. It seemed to be the only choice I had.

We soon heard the buzzing of the helicopter above us. It was landing. The first shuttle to the airstrip consisted of our luggage and the three oldest children. "Paul," I said. "Mommy may have to leave you with Elisabeth and David at the airstrip. Mommy has to go to the hospital with Daddy. Will you watch David and Elisabeth and make sure they do not wander away?

Don't go with anyone except Karen and Paul. They will come soon to get you." Paul seemed as though he understood, but he was only five years old. Was it fair of me to give him such responsibility? I kissed and hugged each of them as they bravely boarded the helicopter. Tears began to stream down my cheeks as I watched them disappear from my sight. It was the first time I had been separated from them. How could I leave them? How long would it be before I saw them again? Would I see them again?

I'm glad I didn't have much time to dwell on those questions. The helicopter soon returned. Warren, still in excruciating pain, was carried by stretcher and put on board. It was a matter of minutes before we arrived at the airstrip and our waiting plane. As we raced to load the plane, my eye caught a glimpse of our three children in the distance standing on a small hill. Paul, five years old, had his arm around David (at that time just four) who in turn had his arm around Elisabeth, who was just two years old. How I struggled with the thought of leaving them! I was their mother. They needed me. But these thoughts kept going through my mind: "Warren needs me. I am his wife—in sickness and in health, till death us do part." My first responsibility was my husband.

Warren was in the plane and the pilot signaled for me to board. I was torn: was I a mother first or a wife first? I wanted to run to my children, but a stronger impulse caused me to turn my head, and not look back. As I boarded that plane, I entrusted my children to the Lord's keeping.

The airstrip where I left them was not an airport with buildings or people around. It was a flat piece of ground, carved out of the bush, on which planes landed—that was it. There were no McDonald's restaurants; no gas stations with restrooms or drinking fountains; no neat little places to hide from the blistering sun. This was the bush of New Guinea—certainly uncivilized by our standards.

You may or may not agree with the decision I made that day. It was something I had to do, and God in His grace gave me the necessary strength. God did protect my children from danger. Karen and Paul arrived about two hours later and found a crowd of people congregated around the children, laughing and having a good time. Paul, David, and Elisabeth were the entertainment for the day. Their singing, dancing, and other crazy antics pleased the Ipili people. God had provided for them.

Upon arriving at the hospital, Warren was rushed into surgery. We thank and praise God for sparing his life. For three of the six weeks Warren was at the hospital, I was his private nurse. During this time I began to fall in love with him all over again. He needed me, and I realized how much I needed him. Without the children demanding our attention every moment, we were able to talk for hours, sharing feelings that had been buried for years. He knew I had chosen him. He was first in my life. It was not a question of who I loved more—the children or him. It was really a question of priorities. He was to be the first. I was a wife first—a mother second.

A DAILY CHOICE

Maybe your marriage has never been tested in such a dramatic way, but the choice is before us every day. Do we honor our husbands as we honor the Lord or are we filled with bitterness, resentment, or anger toward them?

The *Amplified Bible* translates 1 Peter 3:2 in this way.

You are to feel for him all that reverence includes—to respect, defer to, revere him; [revere means] to honor, esteem (appreciate, prize), and [in the human sense] adore him; [and adore means] to admire, praise, be devoted to, deeply love and enjoy [your husband].

That's a large order for any wife to fill, and it requires

wisdom to make the right choices. It cannot take place unless you first of all submit to the lordship of Christ in your life. In learning to revere, honor, esteem, adore, praise, love, and be devoted to Jesus, we learn to give these same things to our husbands. We learn how to love our husbands by loving Jesus. That is why it is so important for Jesus to be first in your life above anything else.

You as a couple need to take out time to be alone, whether for a weekend or for dinner. You may think you cannot afford it, but believe me, you cannot afford not to do it. You need to take time to communicate feelings, to make love, and to enjoy each other physically. Just as you need to schedule time alone with the Lord, so you need to schedule time to be alone with your husband. Don't wait for him to make the first move. Surprise him sometime and make reservations at a motel. Buy yourself a pretty nightgown. He will be absolutely amazed and delighted. Learning how to love each other takes time, but it pays off in dividends far greater than your efforts.

TIME FOR THE TWO OF YOU

The two of you need time alone every day. In New Guinea Warren and I were unable to go out on a date away from home, so we had to think of creative ways to be alone. One of the rules we made in our home is that when Mom and Dad are talking, the children are not to interrupt us. To get away from the children, we often met in our bedroom to talk. When we closed the door, the children were allowed to sit outside and wait until we were finished, but they were not to come in.

We often went for walks and had the children walk either in front of us or behind us so that we could talk. The most precious moments of all were the times we spent after supper on our front porch watching the sunsets. The beauty of the evening sent our hearts soaring to the Lord in praise and toward each other in love.

Are you willing to entrust your children to the Lord's keeping? Are you willing to work on that relationship with your husband, placing him first? Your children will not suffer. Just the opposite will take place. Children growing up where the order of the family is secure are happy children. It is one of the best things you can do for them.

This may take a step of faith, especially if you don't feel you love your husband anymore or if you feel as though you are unappreciated and taken advantage of. Ask God to give you a heart of compassion and love for your husband, a heart that looks beyond his faults to see the strengths that attracted you to him in the first place. Aren't they still there? When you choose to place your husband before your children and yourself, you will be in God's will and blessings will follow.

This is not an easy lesson to learn. The Lord knows how much we rebel and yet His mercy, love, and strength are there for each of us to draw on. Take up the challenge and see what God has waiting for you. Order in your home will produce order in your life.

Chapter 11

No One Can
Do It All

T he birth of a baby into a home of four busy teenagers
and a mother and father approaching middle age
brought many adjustments. The complexion of our home
changed after Danny's birth. A high chair, cradle, playpen, and
other baby items now found their place in our already crowded
home. We made changes daily as we adjusted our lives to meet
the demands of this tiny gift of God.

As awkward at times as our teenagers were about showing
love to one another and to their parents, they freely exhibited
love to Danny. His dependence on them helped them feel loved
and needed. They looked forward to seeing him when they
came home from school. When they felt down, he was always
ready to give them the hugs they needed. Observing this
interaction, I thanked God for the blessings He gave our family
through Danny.

Along with the positive effects came the reality of the estimated 40 percent increase in work a new baby brings. Just
because I had a baby did not mean my life abruptly stopped. I
still had four active teenagers. There was still carpooling to do,

extracurricular activities to attend, and moody temperaments to deal with. My teens needed me now more than ever.

My once orderly house began to take on the look of my confused state. Not only had I become lax in performing daily and weekly duties, I also was too lenient in requiring help from my children. It just took too much energy to convince them of the necessity of doing their required daily jobs.

A FRIENDLY CHALLENGE

Several days before Christmas, a friend who had attended my classes on "Time Management for the Busy Mother" unexpectedly visited our home. With some hesitation, I invited her in. The house was in its typical state of disarray. The kitchen table had not been cleared from lunch; breakfast and lunch dishes were still in the sink; and four pairs of children's shoes were scattered on the family-room floor. To add to my embarrassment, my four older children were watching their favorite TV program, appearing very content with the mess which surrounded them.

With the TV blaring and Danny screaming in my arms, I tried to make my friend feel as comfortable as possible. Sensing my uneasiness, she took Danny from me while I cleared a clean spot at the kitchen table. Quickly I began to explain my problem. "Only two more days, and Christmas will be here, and look at me. My house is a mess. I can't get anything done. You would think with four grown kids to help, this place would be spotless."

She listened sympathetically as I lamented. "You know, kids are all basically the same. They usually won't volunteer to do any work. Teenagers especially seem to thrive in clutter. It doesn't bother them the way it bothers us." Then she began to chuckle. "Somewhere, I remember a woman by the name of Elise teaching a group of women those very principles."

My own words were coming back to haunt me. "Disciplined

mom means disciplined kids," is what I would preach. It made sense. I was the one who had let up. I had not taken the time to delegate and use my authority as their mother. They were unaware of my problem. The house looked great as far as they were concerned.

Even though my children had been taught the value of working at home, the teen years seemed to wipe out all they had learned. Why fold clothes if you are going to wear them right away? Why make the bed if you are going to sleep in it that night? They tried to convince me these tasks were concocted by mothers who wanted to keep their children busy and out of trouble. These chores were a waste of time as far as they were concerned, especially when life was so full of more interesting things to do.

MOM THE MARTYR

Instead of insisting my children help out, I began to play the role of the martyred mom, who says, "I would rather do it myself than listen to your excuses and complaining." Instead of expressing her need for help, she sinks into silence and self-pity.

In the early years of our marriage Warren and I had considerable conflict in this area. It seemed that every time I wanted to clean the house, he wanted to watch TV. I got so irritated seeing him lying on the couch while I worked. Playing the martyr, I slammed cupboard doors, grumbled under my breath, and purposely vacuumed under his feet just to let him know I was working hard and he wasn't. Finally, he would say, "What's your problem?"

I would tearfully respond, "Can't you see? I have so much work to do and you don't even volunteer to help me."

"Elise, all you have to do is ask me to help. I don't know when things need to be done or how to do them."

At first I thought he was using that as an excuse to get out of working, but the more I examined it the more I realized the truth in what he was saying. My husband was not a mind reader. Because our home was not his arena of work, he honestly didn't know what needed to be done. All I had to do was ask in a loving way without nagging and he would willingly help me.

My children were very much the same. They needed to be told in a loving but firm way that I needed help. I could not expect them to volunteer. They needed to be reminded that I was their mother and they were under my authority.

I was glad my friend challenged me to ask for help from my children. Instead of feeling hopeless, I had a new desire to put into action what I had taught them all along about household chores.

A MOTHER'S WORK IS NEVER DONE

With the surge in our society in numbers of single parents and working mothers, there is even more need for family members to chip in and help. Despite our claims to freedom through women's liberation, women are still primarily responsible for child care and household duties. Statistics have shown that women who work outside the home still fix an average of 3 out of 4 meals and do 72 percent of all other household chores. In families where both parents work, the father fixes dinner only 1 night in 16 and the children do it once a week. Many husbands who promised to pitch in with household duties fall woefully short of the mark. For many working women it is a no-win situation. It is not only women who work outside the home who experience this double work load. Mothers who volunteer their services in the community, church, or children's schools may find they may as well be holding down two jobs.

Under these circumstances it is nearly impossible for any mother to function properly unless she receives help. Women who are financially able are increasingly finding the answer in

paid housekeepers. Either way you need to learn the secret of
delegation in the family. If you don't, you will rob yourself of
valuable time and deny your children the privilege of learning
to work.

The biblical pattern is 6/7 work and 1/7 rest (Ex. 20:9-10).
Larry Christianson, author of *The Christian Family*, believes
that 80 percent of a child's waking hours should be spent
working. The average child spends 10 hours of each day sleep-
ing, leaving 14 hours for various activities. If a child spends 6
hours in school, 1 hour doing homework, 3 hours doing chores
and getting ready for school, and 1 hour eating supper, this still
leaves 3 hours (about 20% of his or her waking hours) to play.

DELEGATE!

Moses experienced the same thing as many mothers do today:
too much to do by himself. In Exodus 18 we see Jethro, Moses'
father-in-law, giving advice to Moses.

> Now when Moses' father-in-law saw all that he was doing
> for the people, he said, "What is this thing that you are
> doing for the people? Why do you alone sit as judge and all
> the people stand about you from morning until evening?"
> ... "You will surely wear out, both yourself and these
> people who are with you, for the task is too heavy for you;
> you cannot do it alone.... Select out of all the people
> able men who fear God ... and you shall place these over
> them, as leaders of thousands, of hundreds, of fifties and
> of tens. And let them judge the people at all times; and let
> it be that every major dispute they will bring to you, but
> every minor dispute they themselves will judge. So it will
> be easier for you, and they will bear the burden with you."
> (Ex. 18:14, 21-22)

Business managers know the importance of job delegation.

Time-management experts challenge managers to make lists of all their tasks and ask themselves these two questions: What am I doing that doesn't have to be done? What am I doing that could be handled by someone else?

As home managers we need to ask the same questions. Make lists of daily and weekly jobs. On the daily list, you'll have chores such as setting the table, washing dishes, and making beds. On the weekly list, you may have dusting furniture, vacuuming, and watering plants. Make another list of extra jobs, jobs that can be put off for a certain amount of time, but must be tended to eventually, like washing windows and walls and cleaning the garage, basement, cupboards, and closets.

As you go through your list, consider whether there are daily tasks that you could do weekly and weekly jobs that could be done once a month. Maybe you insist furniture must be moved every time you vacuum; you may decide that this need be done only occasionally. As you go through your lists, you should also begin to see what jobs can be handled by someone else.

Delegating will use more total time in the beginning. Cleaning a bathroom takes me 20 minutes. Having one of my children do it, in the beginning, takes twice as long. We must resist the temptation to do it ourselves. Your impatience will rob you of time later.

In the beginning your children will also not be able to do the job as well as you. Beds will be made on the diagonal, windows will be streaked, and kitchen counters will still have crumbs on them. Don't let your perfection rob you of time later.

When Johnny was about four years old, he decided to make his bed. Terribly proud of his work, he called me into his room to admire it. It was pretty good for a four-year-old's first attempt. As I was praising him, I noticed a big bump in the middle of the bed. "Are those your pj's?" I asked. "No," he replied. "It's only the cat."

Making kids do something they do not want to do is not easy.

They will sometimes make us feel like the meanest moms in the whole world, but mothers are not out to win popularity contests. We are in the process of training children to become healthy, well-adjusted adults. This is a serious undertaking.

Not too long ago, I had an encounter with my four-year-old. I insisted that he pick up his toys, and he refused. In the end I won, but he wasn't going to let me off easily. He looked me square in the eye and said, "You know I don't like you." I said, "You don't have to like me. I'm your mother."

BENEFITS OF WORK

Through work children gain healthier images of themselves. It's a bother sometimes to let a three-year-old vacuum the rug or help bake a pie, but it's not a waste of time. Whenever a child feels a sense of accomplishment, his or her roots of responsibility are growing stronger. Children need to believe in their own ability to make a significant contribution. Work builds up the worker.

Working together as the family builds family unity. It teaches children that they can be active participants in family life. Families that work together are close families. Each member feels needed. Our family shares many fond memories of times we all chipped in and worked on a major project around the house, like painting a room or doing spring or fall yard work. We worked together, and we had fun.

Work opens the door to communication. In the days before dishwashers, washing dishes was a time for talk as well as work. Even in silence communication takes place. By working with our children, we are sharing with them some of the deepest, most important values of life. Becoming responsible adults is not simply a matter of hanging up pajamas or putting dirty towels in the hamper, but caring about ourselves and others and seeing everyday chores as related to how we treat this world that God so beautifully created.

GUIDELINES FOR DELEGATING

I recommend that mothers begin to teach their children early to work. Even the youngest child can learn to pick up toys after playing. Toddlers can be trained to put away their shoes, fetch things for Mother, and empty wastebaskets. Each one of my children had his very own spray bottle of Windex. They loved cleaning windows, the refrigerator, and stove.

Be sure to delegate only one job at a time. Most children can only handle one command at a time. As they get older and are used to working, they may be able to do several things in sequence.

Do not give in to their complaints and grumbling. I don't know very many children who respond with joy when their mother asks them to work. When my children complained, I just told them that work builds character and that God will bless them. I need to remind them they are not just working for me but also for God. "Whether, then, you eat or drink or whatever you do, do all to the glory of God" (1 Cor. 10:31).

Yelling, screaming, and nagging sometimes motivates kids to work, but I don't recommend it. It wears you out; it degrades the children; and it destroys the closeness you are trying to build. You receive more respect and get better results if you speak firmly, ignore their complaining and arguments, and follow through with what you have said.

Be as positive as you possibly can about work. Explain how good they will feel about themselves when their work is finished. They will be proud of themselves. When my children's rooms are clean, they spend more time in them. They stop to admire the windows they have just washed and the lawn they have just mowed. After mowing and trimming the lawn one day, David stepped back to admire his work. I happened to be outside and complimented him on the fine job. "You know," he said, "someday I might think about going into the landscaping business." It made him feel good to do a job well.

RESPECT YOUR YOUNG WORKERS

Children are to be obedient to their parents in all things, but Scripture also reminds parents not to exasperate or provoke our children to anger "that they may not lose heart" (Col. 2:20-21). We are not to purposefully put more on our children than they are capable of handling. Some children are more skillful or mechanical, while others need jobs that call for more repetition. Give them tasks that match their abilities.

Our children are not our slaves, and we are not to be angry taskmasters. That is why working with them is so important, especially in the beginning. We show them we are all in this together.

It is also wise to plan out a work schedule ahead of time. Make out a list ahead of time and post it on the refrigerator. Children need goals as much as adults do. They need to know what jobs need to be done, how long it will take, and who is assigned to do what.

Warren and I have learned to set time limits for the work we require from our children. No one likes to work all day. On Saturdays each child gives us just two hours of his or her time. After the allotted time, they are free for the rest of the day. During the summer, we set aside mornings each day for doing chores. If everything gets done as planned, we reward them with an afternoon treat, like a trip to the park, beach, or local ice-cream parlor. Sometimes we play Monopoly, have a baseball game, or go to a movie.

Be sure to praise your children as they work, even if the job is not done to your specifications. Try to find something good about it. Your compliments will spur them on to do it even better the next time. Tell them how proud you are of their determination to get the job done. Next time, work with them and help in the areas that need improvement.

Allow for mistakes. David once washed a red sweatshirt with a load of his white clothes and ended up with pink underwear.

It was funny to his brothers, but devastating to him. He learned a hard lesson, and he hasn't repeated the mistake since. Confusing hair spray for Windex or boiling potatoes in a pan that is too small are all natural mistakes. Don't be too hard on your kids. Correct but don't punish them for these errors.

ALLOWANCES

Should children be paid to do jobs required of them as part of the family? If they do their jobs and do them faithfully, without constant reminders and complaining, and do them well, I feel allowances are good. Most children receive allowances they don't deserve, which doesn't help them. Instead it teaches them to expect something without having to put forth any effort.

Our children did not receive weekly allowances. Instead, we paid them for doing specific jobs. If I wanted walls washed, I paid them a certain amount for each wall. I paid Elisabeth to iron her dad's shirts. Cleaning the garage and washing the windows were extra jobs, for which I would pay them small fees. Jobs they were to do on a regular basis (such as taking out the trash, doing dishes, vacuuming, dusting, cutting the lawn, cleaning their rooms, and washing their clothes) were their contribution to family living, so no pay was given.

BUILDING FOR THE FUTURE

My children have all learned to share in the responsibility of living in a family. They have all learned to care for their rooms and clothing (washing, folding, and ironing). They know how to vacuum, dust, and sweep floors, and now, with the addition of Danny, even change diapers. Because they have taken over many responsibilities in our home, I am free to serve the Lord through my writing, conference speaking, and ministry at our church. I could not do it without their help and support. The years of training them were difficult and time consuming, but now I'm reaping the benefits. Someday my son-in-law and daughters-in-law will appreciate my perseverance. They will have husbands and a wife who have learned the benefits of work.

You are doing a disservice to your children and to yourself if you are not teaching them how to work. They will learn some of life's most valuable lessons through work, their self-esteem will be elevated, and you will find greater freedom.

Chapter 12

Moving On!

I t is an interesting fact of nature that growth usually takes place in seclusion and silence—a baby in the womb, seeds buried beneath the soil, butterflies encased in their cocoons. In seclusion, they are being transformed. Nothing can hurry the process. At just the right time, they emerge from their protected, silent places, in all of God's intended beauty.

A pearl is formed when a grain of sand or some irritant becomes lodged between the shell and mantle of a mollusk. The irritation causes the mantle to coat the invading object with layers of a substance called mother of pearl. Hidden in darkness and silence, this speck of sand receives layer upon layer of this exquisite pearly substance, and it is transformed into a pearl of great worth. At just the right time, a diver will discover this pearl of great worth and release it from its place of seclusion.

A MOTHER'S GROWTH
Many mothers feel like that speck of sand trapped in the shell of the oyster. Very little seems to be happening around us. Those years of child rearing are years of seclusion. Judging from

outward appearances, nothing seems to be transpiring. Life is ordinary and routine; we feel isolated from reality and society.

In the midst of ordinary tasks and irritations, though, tremendous growth is taking place. In seclusion, God is preparing us for the day when we will move from service within our homes to service outside our homes. We are learning each day what it means to live and act as Christians. The Holy Spirit is our private tutor as we learn forgiveness, love, servanthood, and prayer. To faith is being added excellence, knowledge, self-control, perseverance, godliness, brotherly kindness, and Christian love (2 Peter 1:5-7). Jesus gently layers us with His love, giving us His mind. He is the one who molds and fashions us into something beautiful. We are being transformed from specks of sand into lovely pearls.

In Acts 8 we read about a man in a vibrant, mainstream ministry in Samaria. Great crowds listened to Philip preach, and they heeded what he was saying. This man of God performed miracles, signs, and wonders. In the midst of this, Philip received a message from an angel of the Lord to leave Samaria and go to Gaza along a desert road. In his obedience to God, he doesn't walk, he runs to this place (Acts 8:30). There he finds an Ethiopian eunuch reading from the Prophet Isaiah. Philip explains the Scriptures, leads the man to Christ, and baptizes him. Then Philip is miraculously snatched away by the Spirit of the Lord and returned once again to his ministry of preaching the Gospel (8:39-40).

Like Philip, many of us have been taken out of the mainstream of life to take on motherhood. Those years seem endless, but soon God will move us into the world. Many of us lack patience. We want motherhood, a career, social involvement, and well-behaved, grown-up children all at once. The process God chooses takes time.

Knowing the right time to move from the family situation to the world outside the home has everything to do with priorities. When a woman's priorities are lined up with God's will, there is a natural progression that takes place. A woman's relationship with the Lord leads her to function properly in her family. Eventually service outside her home will become a part of her life.

WEIGHING THE OPTIONS

Many become involved outside their home for financial reasons and others for self-gratification. Whatever the motive, choices should be weighed and considered in the light of God's will. Unless we are in the will of God, time will become our greatest enemy.

As a mother of four young children, I never envisioned myself as an author of two books or a conference speaker and Bible teacher. My credentials—wife of Rev. Warren Arndt, mother of five children, and former missionary to New Guinea—weren't too impressive from a worldly point of view. But God is an expert at taking the foolishness of the world and turning it into His wisdom. In His time God has moved me from my home situation to serve Him in the world, but only after I learned to put Him first and my family second. He wanted me to learn my lessons well in the life of my family before He used me in the world.

Opportunities for service and work outside my home are constantly beckoning. Just recently I was offered a position at one of Detroit's Christian radio stations. I was flattered; I felt honored and humbled to think that God could use me in such a way. In my mind I thought of the number of people I would be able to reach every day with the Gospel message. My ministry to women and helping them with their children could be expanded. Practically speaking it seemed beneficial to my family. With three children in college and one in a private high school, we could have used the financial help.

My immediate impulse was to take the job, but I have learned to wait on the Lord. The desire of my life is to do the will of my Heavenly Father. This decision would affect not only me, but also my entire family. My four older children were well on their way to maturity, but I still had Danny, who was only four years old. He still depended on me a great deal.

As Warren and I prayed, we asked the Lord for direction. While attending a church conference in Florida, I was able to share my predicament with a few pastors in hopes of receiving wisdom. It seemed as if I was not getting anywhere, until one of them said, "You know, Elise, your husband is vulnerable without you. He needs you at his side emotionally, spiritually, and physically."

I laughed and commented, "You mean the place where God took the rib out of man to make woman is weak and needs protection?" As I said that, I put my arms around Warren and stood close to him. I was reminded of Ecclesiastes 4:9-12.

Two are better than one because they have a good return for their labor. For if either of them falls, the one will lift up his companion. But woe to the one who falls when there is not another to lift him up. Furthermore, if two lie down together they keep warm, but how can one be warm alone? And if one can overpower him who is alone, two can resist him. A cord of three strands is not quickly torn apart.

I was concerned for my children, but at this point in our lives, Warren needed me too. I chose to be a wife first, and a career woman second. Those are tough words in our day of women's liberation. But could it be that the reason many marriages are disintegrating is that women are placing other things before their husbands and children? I was called to be Warren's "helpmeet." It was not the right time for me to move on. I was to wait on the Lord.

MOVING WITH THE LORD

Shortly after turning down this job offer, Exodus 40:34-37 caught my attention.

> Then the cloud [the Shekinah, God's visible presence] covered the tent of meeting, and the glory of the Lord filled the tabernacle. And Moses was not able to enter the tent of meeting because the cloud had settled on it, and the glory of the Lord filled the tabernacle. And throughout all their journeys whenever the cloud was taken up from over the tabernacle, the sons of Israel would set out; but if the cloud was not taken up, then they did not set out until the day when it was taken up.

In my spiritual notebook I wrote these words:

> Moses was given explicit directions in the building of the tabernacle. . . . When all was finished the Shekinah glory of the Lord filled that place.
> So it is with our lives as mothers. We work in our homes to get things in order. We operate according to the Holy Spirit's direction. When all is in order the glory of the Lord fills our homes. But we must be careful not to leave that place *until God moves us*.
> Israel was not to move without the Shekinah glory of the Lord moving first. Should it be any different in our lives? If I move before God moves, will His glory go with me? The glory of the Lord is dwelling in my home. . . . There will be a time when it will move out and I will know. To move without the presence of God would be foolishness.

ESCAPING PROBLEMS

Your motives for entering into employment, volunteer positions, and ministry should always be examined carefully. The world tells us to leave the scene of a troubled marriage or disorganized home. If you are not appreciated by anyone, seek recognition, we are told.

If your home is not in order, working is not going to solve the problem. You will still come home to an irate husband, undisciplined children, and a messy house. These things do not dissipate while you are absent; they only get worse. You will have less time and energy to work at remedying your situation.

I have often wanted to escape from my present situation. I have neglected my family to pursue my own wants and desires. I thank and praise God for always drawing me back to reexamine my priorities and then giving me the fortitude to stick to them. Whenever my priorities have been out of line, I have wasted time. When my priorities are out of line, my family is the first to suffer. I have seen the look of rejection on my children's faces when I have chosen my ministry and work above them and their needs. When I place God first in my life, my family second, and my work and ministry third, I am at peace.

SERVING AT CHURCH RATHER THAN AT HOME
Many Christian women fall into the trap of equating ministry with relationship with God. They place ministry above the family. I know women whose homes are in physical, spiritual, or emotional disorder (sometimes all three), and yet they insist that serving the Lord comes before serving their families. They teach Bible studies, serve on church committees, and prepare church dinners, but they put aside the "apron of humility" as they enter their homes. Tired and exhausted from serving the Lord outside their homes, they are unable to serve Him in their homes. No matter how much people need us outside our homes, we must keep before us the fact that our families come first.

Warren and I have witnessed many children who are rebelling because their mothers and fathers do not have time for them. They feel slighted because of their parents' involvement in church, and they grow up resenting it. Overinvolvement in ministry can result in such demanding schedules that there is little time for communication, laughter, and fun with family members. This is not God's intent. He desires our service to be done in joy. He wants our children to imitate us in service, not spurn ministry to Him. Warren and I are both involved in ministry outside our home. We have to continually evaluate how this is affecting our family. The Lord spoke to my heart many years ago about becoming too involved in things outside my home. "What will it profit you, Elise, if you gain the whole world for Christ and lose your own children?" What would it profit me, if I earned a great salary and was able to buy them everything they wanted, but could not give them my time?

DOING TOO MUCH

The time does come in a woman's life when the Lord begins to move her into areas outside her home. As the kids begin school, a mother may investigate part-time employment, involvement in school activities, teaching Bible studies, and so on. But she must beware of becoming too involved.

Children will not come right out and tell you they miss your presence at home. Changes in sleep patterns, recurring nightmares or bad dreams, unusual fears, nail biting, bed wetting, a return to thumb sucking, and wanting a bottle after being weaned could all be signs that your child misses you. Be sensitive to your children and aware of their behavior.

Once when I was doing a radio talk show, a young mother called in seeking help for a problem with her four-year-old son. He was wetting his bed after being trained for almost two years and he wanted to have a bottle. Upon questioning, I found she was a single parent. She obviously did not have the choice of staying home, but she did have a choice in another area. Within the past three months she had decided to go back to school to improve her chances for a better job. Because she left her little boy in the care of sitters in the evening, he began to show his disapproval. He was in effect saying to her, "Mom, I need you. I miss you."

Going to school was a way of improving herself and bolstering their financial security. Others admired her for the sacrifices she was making. I challenged her to rethink what was really important. Could going back to school wait? Did she have to take several courses at one time? Would it be better to take just one course each semester instead of two? There were alternatives. Her little boy needed her now. She needed to look beyond her own wants and on to what God wanted from her. There would be plenty of time for her to complete her education, but right now that little boy was of greater importance.

EVALUATING POTENTIAL ACTIVITIES

How do I determine my involvement outside the home? The first question I consider is whether my involvement will interfere with the time I need to spend with God. It seems that the busier we are the less time we spend with God, even though, as we have seen, what we need is *more* time with God. If I take on a new activity, will I be willing to spend more time with the Lord or will work schedules prevent me from having daily fellowship with Him? It can be done. I know extremely busy women who schedule special time each day with the Lord. But it has not come easy and they must sacrifice something.

The second thing I think about is how much actual time I will be spending away from my family. I have to take into consideration traveling to and from my destination and any preparation time at home. Will I still be able to be with my husband and kids when they need me?

What about the emotional energy required? Fifteen minutes

spent on the phone counseling can at times wipe me out emotionally for the rest of the day. Working on a volunteer committee may only use up two hours, but the emotional energy expended may count for eight hours. I must evaluate what I am doing by the amount of emotional energy it requires.

Something else I need to consider is the amount of support I can count on from my family. When a woman first considers work outside the home, family members usually promise to help out at home, but after a while Mother finds herself holding down two jobs.

How much should a Christian woman be involved in her church if she has a husband who is not saved? This question is asked over and over by women who have an honest desire to serve the Lord but feel they are hindered by their husbands. A woman in this situation should ask herself, "Does my husband resent my involvement?" If he does, she will be fighting a losing battle. I suggest to these women that they be very cautious. There are many opportunities during the day to serve the Lord while your husband is at work. You may also have to work harder to make sure the house is in order and meals are ready on time, because if these are neglected, your husband may blame your involvement at church. Pray and ask for God's will to be revealed.

One area women often fail to examine when seeking employment or taking on added activities outside the home is how this is going to affect the ministry to which God has called them in their churches. Women's Bible studies, even the ones offered in the evening, have declined over the years. Sunday and midweek school teachers are scarce. Part of the reason for this is the rise in the number of women working. Little time is left for church activities. We need to seriously consider how added activities will affect the ministry to which we have been called by the Holy Spirit.

Every Christian woman should also discover where she is

most gifted by the Holy Spirit. I used to feel I had to be all things to all people. As a result, I served on committees for church dinners, made evangelism calls, visited nursing homes, taught Sunday School and Bible classes during the week. When I learned that the Holy Spirit gives gifts to the body of Christ (Rom. 12:4-8, 1 Cor. 12:4-31; Eph. 4:4-12) "for the equipping of the saints for the work of service, to the building up of the body of Christ" (Eph. 4:12), I no longer felt compelled to do it all. God had given gifts to others too. By my being involved in so much I was depriving others of the privilege of serving and exercising their gifts.

I began to pray for my spiritual gift or gifts to be revealed. Soon I found myself being blessed in teaching the Bible to the women at our church. This then became my main area of involvement. I was free to say no to other things, because others could do them far better than I could.

The final question each of us ultimately has to ask is, "Have I sought God's direction or is this something only I want to do?" (Ps. 32:8-9; Prov. 16:3)

CHOOSING GOD'S BEST

After Danny was born, I felt like Philip must have when he was compelled to travel the desert road. Taken out of the mainstream of activity and a vibrant ministry, I was removed to the desert of my home. For the sake of one (and really my entire family) God called me to do this. I did not want to run to obey as Philip did. I dragged my feet. My world seemed to be passing me by. I was at an age where babies belonged to my past, not my future. My friends had children who were all grown, and they were excited about venturing into careers or going back to school. Friends who were teachers and authors were speaking and traveling. Their popularity increased, while mine seemed to decrease. I longed for the greener pastures on the other side. At times I rebelled against God for allowing my life to come to a screeching halt, but my commitment to motherhood has been strong, and I know I have made the right decision. Deep in my heart I know God is in control and that His appointed time will be there for me. As I seek His direction, He begins to lead me into other areas of ministry.

God has not whisked me back into the mainstream of activity as quickly or as supernaturally as He did Philip. I have been in seclusion and quiet for almost five years. The Lord has had much for me to learn during this time. I have been layered with His love. From a speck of sand I am being formed into something lovely and useful for the kingdom of God.

Slowly I am being led back into ministry. The choices before me in serving God outside my home are not choices between good and bad. They are choices between what is good and what is best.